## CORNWALL

Edited by
Dave Thomas

GW00500474

First published in Great Britain in 1998 by
*POETRY NOW YOUNG WRITERS*
1-2 Wainman Road, Woodston,
Peterborough, PE2 7BU
Telephone (01733) 230748

HB ISBN 0 75430 125 7
SB ISBN 0 75430 126 5

# FOREWORD

With over 63,000 entries for this year's Cosmic competition, it has proved to be our most demanding editing year to date.

We were, however, helped immensely by the fantastic standard of entries we received, and, on behalf of the Young Writers team, thank you.

The Cosmic series is a tremendous reflection on the writing abilities of 8-11 year old children, and the teachers who have encouraged them must take a great deal of credit.

We hope that you enjoy reading *Cosmic Cornwall* and that you are impressed with the variety of poems and style with which they are written, giving an insight into the minds of young children and what they think about the world today.

# CONTENTS

| | |
|---|---|
| Rebecca Brooks | 18 |
| Oliver Whiting | 19 |
| Matthew Lodey | 19 |
| Lucy Frost | 20 |
| Verity Stephan | 20 |

**Bodriggy Primary School**

| | |
|---|---|
| Natalie Richardson | 21 |
| Hannah Saunders | 21 |
| Jenny Dawn Ritchie | 22 |
| Hannah Smith | 22 |
| Christopher Williams | 23 |
| Jason Sparks | 23 |
| Daniel Orchard | 24 |
| Amy Ellis | 24 |
| Corinne Homer | 25 |
| Craig Rennard | 25 |
| Kerenza Berry | 26 |
| Chloe Amber Frost | 26 |
| Benjamin Peters | 27 |
| Max Bell | 27 |
| Samuel McBride | 28 |
| Colette Hawker | 28 |
| Scott Gunn | 29 |

**Boskenwyn CP School**

| | |
|---|---|
| Nicholas Hort | 29 |
| Katie Pedley | 29 |
| Alexander Hort | 30 |
| Jinny Wadsworth | 30 |
| Aine Bailey | 31 |
| Julio Birch | 31 |
| Louise Williams | 31 |
| Simoné Foreman | 32 |
| Peter Symms | 32 |

Callington CP School

| | |
|---|---|
| Catherine Mutton | 32 |
| Louise Hatton | 33 |
| Karl Langman | 33 |
| Steven Pound | 33 |
| Kathryn Skelton | 34 |
| Cara Bowers | 34 |
| Rebecca Leverington | 34 |
| Philip Stephens | 35 |
| Sarah Moir | 35 |
| Kayleigh Wheatley | 36 |
| Jade Turner | 36 |
| Samantha Biggs | 37 |
| Katie Williams | 37 |
| Lea-Anne Ansell | 38 |
| Adam Holloway | 38 |
| Serena Skews | 39 |
| Kathy Mackrory | 39 |

Camborne St Meriadoc CE Junior School

| | |
|---|---|
| Tom West | 40 |
| Jake Smith | 41 |

Calstock CP School

| | |
|---|---|
| Rebecca Williams | 42 |
| Robin Williams | 42 |
| Lamorna Elmer | 43 |
| Samantha Davies | 43 |
| Amy Elmer | 44 |
| Elizabeth Crowell | 44 |
| Madeline Amy Spurr | 45 |
| Joanna Smith | 45 |
| Harry Barnett | 46 |
| Rachael Shayer | 46 |
| Leigh-Anne Alford | 47 |
| Kai Kenyon | 47 |
| William Shayer | 47 |
| Laurie Mason Kaye | 48 |

| | |
|---|---|
| Micayla Barnet | 48 |
| Emma Clay | 48 |
| Matthew Wilson | 49 |
| James Vaughan | 49 |
| Stephanie Hobbs | 49 |
| Emma Price | 50 |
| Vanessa Hemmett | 50 |
| Laura Stephens | 50 |
| Alexandra Allden | 51 |
| Rachel Fowler | 51 |
| Christopher Crowell | 51 |
| Christopher Nance | 52 |
| Francesca Hannon | 52 |
| Kevin Pethick | 53 |
| Sam Leonard Williams | 53 |
| Kit Kaye | 53 |
| Clare Edmunds | 54 |

**Chacewater CP School**

| | |
|---|---|
| Charlotte Brand | 54 |
| Ben Sowden | 55 |
| Rory Dunham | 55 |
| Sarah Lane | 56 |
| Tanya Johns | 56 |
| Sarah Brooks | 57 |
| Lucy J Heffer | 57 |
| Adalean Coade | 57 |
| Jordan Hamilton | 58 |
| Christopher Turner | 58 |
| Amy Jose | 59 |
| David Tamblyn | 59 |
| Alishea Buck | 59 |
| Martha Whitfield | 60 |
| Alice Hunter | 60 |
| Victoria Ball | 61 |

| | |
|---|---|
| Kevin Hatch | 79 |
| Thomas Arrowsmith | 79 |
| Joseph Pooley | 79 |
| Tom Potts | 80 |
| Emma Woodridge | 80 |
| Leanne Williams | 81 |
| Michael Diebner | 81 |
| Matthew Parnall | 82 |
| Timothy Strong | 82 |
| Karl Woodridge | 83 |
| David Striplin | 83 |
| Lucy Addicott | 84 |
| Kenny Channing | 84 |
| Thomas Brown | 85 |
| Joshua Hall | 85 |
| Thomas Adams | 86 |
| Edward Horn | 87 |
| Nathan Jones | 87 |
| Georgina Freestone | 88 |
| Wayne Richter | 88 |
| Amy Gathercole | 89 |
| Lorna White | 90 |
| Steven Smith | 90 |
| Geraldine Harris | 91 |

Liskeard Junior School

| | |
|---|---|
| Cassie Rowe | 91 |
| Axie Lavers | 92 |
| Lucy Rigby | 92 |
| Ben Williams | 93 |
| Heather Butt | 93 |
| Lucy Williams | 94 |
| Jamie Julian | 94 |
| Daniel Broster | 95 |
| Guy Stroud | 95 |
| Peter Little | 96 |
| Tamsin Job | 96 |
| Adrian Vine | 97 |

St Columb Major CP School

| | |
|---|---|
| Ben Atherton | 188 |
| Tom Davey | 188 |
| Rachelle Forrest | 189 |
| Gemma Hall | 190 |
| Briony Chapman | 190 |
| Laura J Dolan | 191 |
| Janine Lawer | 192 |
| Laura Perry | 192 |
| Simon Riley | 193 |
| Helen Jones | 194 |
| Kimberley Bazeley | 194 |
| Vicky Tremain | 195 |
| Clare Jenkin | 195 |
| Katie Varcoe | 196 |
| Laura Davies | 197 |
| Jane Wood | 197 |
| Rebecca Shephard | 198 |
| Tessa Crawford | 199 |
| Aaron Rundle | 200 |
| Gemma Davis | 201 |
| Alice Brenton | 202 |

St Erme With Trispen CP School, Truro

| | |
|---|---|
| Craig James | 202 |
| Zoe Rawicki | 203 |
| Chloe Hart | 204 |
| Nicola Hawke | 204 |
| Kieran Cooper | 205 |
| Jen Saywell | 206 |
| Freya Coglan | 206 |
| Lisa Reeks | 207 |
| Thomas Connell | 207 |
| Aimie Cole | 208 |
| Bethany Key | 209 |
| Danielle Penny | 210 |
| Laura Jones | 210 |

St Hilary CP School, Truro

| | |
|---|---|
| Tom Somers | 211 |
| Kate Hamilton | 212 |
| William Prior | 212 |
| Viv Ziar | 213 |
| Mark Hammond | 214 |
| Maree Smith | 214 |
| Katie Scrase | 215 |
| Emma Williams | 215 |
| Briony Berryman | 216 |
| Holly Bowden | 216 |
| Louise Hardcastle | 217 |
| Tracy Kessell | 218 |
| Stephanie Lawrence | 218 |
| Ben Walker | 219 |
| Steven Burt | 219 |
| James Preston | 220 |
| Stephanie Jilbert | 220 |
| Tom Robbens | 221 |
| Terry Bryant | 221 |
| Samuel Clemo | 222 |
| Michael Cross | 222 |
| Megan Westley | 223 |
| Jeremy Mepham | 223 |
| Simon Nellist | 224 |
| Jeremy Kent | 225 |

St Ives Junior School

| | |
|---|---|
| Laura Cocking | 225 |
| Amelia Sutherland | 226 |
| Dean Bungay | 227 |
| James Moon | 228 |
| Jamie Bryce | 228 |
| Jacqueline Luckham | 229 |
| Nicholas Quarton-Cats | 229 |
| Christopher Lock | 230 |
| Charlotte Johnson | 230 |
| Luke Tierney | 231 |

| | |
|---|---|
| Marc Sims | 283 |
| Andrew Wills | 283 |
| Holly Williams | 283 |
| Jessie Hands | 284 |
| Ben Oldcorn | 284 |
| Gary Eddy | 285 |
| Jonathan Pollard | 285 |
| Matthew Francis | 286 |
| Liane Keast | 286 |
| Clare Noall | 287 |
| Martin Nicholls | 287 |
| Jennifer Deponeo | 288 |

St Teath School, Bodmin

| | |
|---|---|
| Naomi Smith | 288 |
| Jenna Commins | 289 |
| Lauren Sandercock | 290 |
| Lucy Blewett | 290 |
| Tanya Mountain | 291 |
| Daniel Ede | 292 |

Shortlanesend CP School

| | |
|---|---|
| Sam Langford | 292 |
| Paul Falconbridge | 293 |
| Fay Nicholls | 293 |
| Jane Grylls | 293 |
| Thomas Duncan | 294 |
| Thomas Hinkley | 294 |
| Richard Holroyd | 294 |
| Luke Hegarty | 295 |

Treliske Preparatory School

| | |
|---|---|
| Tim Ballingal | 295 |
| Ben Ackner | 296 |
| Marie Powers | 297 |
| Natalie Gadsby | 298 |
| Rebecca Wills-Devlin | 298 |
| Rachael O'Rourke | 299 |

# THE POEMS

## THE SWAN

The swan is beautifully white
Don't come too close or she will bite.
The swan glides in the skies
Watching everyone with her eyes.
The swan flies down to the ground
Don't disturb her or she will pound, pound, pound.
The beautiful white swan
Pulls up reeds, weed and grasses from the ponds.
The swan is beautifully white
Don't come too close or she will bite.
The baby cygnets are now born
She will take them sightseeing.
To see the beaches and fields of corn.
Then they go back to see the cob
He is sitting on a log,
Looking proud and graceful.

*Danielle Jenkin (11)*
*Alverton CP School*


## THE MUTE SWAN

The enchanting mute swan, flies delicately
Through the fine blue sky, majestic, powerful
Yet swiftly glides through the air like a dolphin
Through the deep long ocean.
A giant amongst birds, yet as agile as the
                                        dwarf-like blue tit,
Both in air and water
She lands from migration for another season,
Then off she goes, above the great white clouds.

*Kir Roberts (11)*
*Alverton CP School*

## TIMMY

Timmy was a dog and he liked to roam the street,
Timmy was a dog and his second name was Pete
Timmy was a dog and he was quite neat,
Timmy was a dog and always got at mum's feet!

Timmy was a dog and was very annoying,
Timmy then again could be quite enjoying,
Timmy was a dog and liked to play catch,
Timmy was a dog and liked a football match.

But sadly one morning, good old Timmy died,
It was very sad and we all began to cry,
But good old Timmy, we still love you!
But now we've got another dog and called it Timmy Too!

*Carl Wakfer  (11)*
*Alverton CP School*


## THE MUTE SWAN

Gliding through the air
The mute swan dances in the wind.
The beautiful bird aims downwards
To reach the sparkling water.
She finds her cygnets
She gently lays the food into the starving mouths
To quench their thirst and hunger.
She then takes off once more
Only to find a poacher
*Bang*
She falls down to instant death
She has finished her long journey at last.

*Paul Sampson  (10)*
*Alverton CP School*

## ALONE

Hello, hello
Is anyone there?
I'm stuck all alone
No friends to play with
Boredom consumes bits of me
Mouthful by mouthful

The playground jumps up at me
'Play with us
Play'

I just ignore their call
I imagine pictures
But all I see is
Games.

Creeping up on me
Forcing me to join
But
I can't.

*Lucy Stubbings (11)*
*Alverton CP School*


## SWANS

Swans are great
Swans are white
Swans are really nice
They may peck
But they don't bite!

*David Hall (10)*
*Alverton CP School*

## SAVING

The sound of a thud
As trees start to fall

Trying to save
We could just do that

We could just sit and relax
But I wouldn't resist

We can save everything
We can do just that

Help us help the world
Save yourselves

And this is a message
To get across to you all

Save this land
Save the world.

*Lauren Williams (9)*
*Alverton CP School*


## THE BEAUTY OF THE SEA

The beauty of the sea is you
Gliding gracefully,
Through and through
Coral reefs,
Black with a white underneath
Splashing
Through and through.

*Morwenna Harris (10)*
*Alverton CP School*

## THE RIVER

I saw a wonderful waterfall,
I saw a waterfall falling out of the trees.

I hear the wind blowing in the trees,
I hear the wind howling.

I can smell the fresh water from the tap,
I can smell the fresh spring season.

I felt the sparkling river,
I felt the powerful water.

I felt as happy as a boy who had been to
                    Disneyland for a day
I felt as happy as a butterfly.

*Sameer Al-Harthy (7)*
*Alverton CP School*


## CARING

Caring is being concerned about someone.
Caring is to take caution of what you
Say so you don't hurt someone's feelings.
Caring is to be aware of people's troubles
                    and to help them
Caring is to take care of your things
Caring is to help people through their troubles
Caring is to help!

*Josie Griffith (11)*
*Alverton CP School*

## THE MUTE SWAN

Silent and graceful,
Quiet and peaceful,
Calm and gentle.

In the air
She's like a twelve kilo jet,
And like a smooth canoe
In the water.

The mute swan
Silent and graceful.

*Jowan Phillips  (11)*
*Alverton CP School*

## TO REACH THE SEA

It was fine
When it was mine
We went past the river
And it nearly caught us for dinner
Leaves were falling
When it was dawning
We went into the forest
And everyone was honest
We went down to a place
And had a boat race
At last we reached the sea
And that's the end of our journey.

*Joel Spiegelhalter  (8)*
*Alverton CP School*

## SAVING

Save the rainforest
Recycle glass and paper
Plastic too
Stop the environment
From being spoiled

Try to stop the dumps filling
And natural resources being lost
Pile up the recycle bins
Make the rubbish bins empty

Recycle all natural resources
'Cause we won't have any left
Stop dumps piling up
Make the world a better place.

*Zoe Roberts (9)*
*Alverton CP School*


## LIGHT AND DARK

Creamy, chalky snow
The sun is shining brightly
Candles in the dark
Orange light brightening the street
The moon is shining at night.

Pitch black in a cave
Darkness creeps around at night
Owls fly silently
Badgers are hunting at night
Silence in the blight at night.

*Daniel Freeman (8)*
*Alverton CP School*

# IN THE DARK

I'm waiting under my covers shivering
My teddy comes alive in the dark
It's black in the dark
Creaking doors in the dark
What's under the bed at night in the dark?

Help mum
There are spooky shadows in the dark
It's a mystery in the dark
It's gloomy in the dark
Ghosts rise from their graves in the dark.

I hear funny noises
It's cold in the dark
Cat's eyes glow in the dark
I hear cats fighting in the dark.

*Addison White (8)*
*Alverton CP School*


# THE BULLY

Once at my old school
One of the bullies came
Kicked me,
My head hit the school wall
When I was in the park
I got hit in the leg
With a metal pole
I got pushed off the see-saw
I felt very upset
My head and knee hurt very much.

*Kathrine Louise Taylor (8)*
*Alverton CP School*

# IN THE DARK

I cannot sleep in the dark
My sister is snoring in the dark
My bedroom comes alive in the dark
There is something under my bed in the dark

I am not alone
I can see something creeping on the floor in the dark
I can hear the cars outside on the road in the dark
I can hear the cats miaow in the dark
Nothing is normal in the dark

All my toys look scary in the dark
I can see my teddy with huge eyes starting at me in the dark
My mummy turns the light off then I am in the dark
In the dark.

*Laura Parsons  (8)*
*Alverton CP School*


# WALKING BACKWARDS

I saw a glistening waterfall,
Shining like a blue crystal

I could smell rotting soil,
I could hear rattling foil

I felt a patch of frost,
Then my hair-band got lost

It was like a miracle come true,
That the sky had turned blue.

*Jessica Ross  (8)*
*Alverton CP School*

## IN THE DARK

Curtains rustling in the dark
My closet doors opening in the dark
Under my bed in the dark
I am shivering in the dark.

A gloomy graveyard in the dark
Ghosts in the dark
Creaking doors in the dark
Lurky figures in the dark
Dark shadows in the dark
Owls hooting in the dark.

Thumping footsteps in the dark
Spooky noises in the dark
Cat's eyes glowing in the dark
It is black in the dark.

*Louise Hobin (8)*
*Alverton CP School*


## THE LIQUORICE ALLSORT

The liquorice allsort
He went to an airport
And jumped on a very big plane
He thought he'd go to France
'I know,' he said 'I'll go to sunny Spain.'
When he got into the hotel he sat on a big chair
And unfortunately he lost all his hair
But he had a good time and some fun
Bye bye, liquorice allsort you've melted away in the sun.

*Jamie Jones (8)*
*Alverton CP School*

## A SPOOK AT NIGHT

It is spooky in the dark
A ghost in the dark
It is black in the dark

A spook in the dark
I have been spooked in the dark
It is spooky at night in the dark

Outside in the dark
The mystery's in the dark
I shiver in the dark

An owl hoots in the dark
Eyes glow in the dark
Why do I shiver in the dark?

I am scared in the dark
Eyes in the dark
A fox in the dark.

*Kailash Kay  (8)*
*Alverton CP School*



## THE SEED

The seed is like a cannon ball
So round and hard
The stem is like a piece of green cotton
The leaves are like a piece of clothing
The petals are like a paper plane.

*Ryan Holland  (7)*
*Alverton CP School*

## THE SEED

The seed is like a baby
Waiting for birth
The roots are like little ropes
Anchoring the treasure down
The shoot is like a little ladder
Climbing to a cloud
The leaves are like little doors
Opening into the tree
The petals are like diamonds
Glittering in the night.

*Rosie Kliskey (7)*
*Alverton CP School*

## THE FLOWERS

The seed is like a drum
Banging away
The roots are like a long stick
Reaching into the ground
The shoot is like legs
Going up into the sky
The leaves are like a paper vase
Flat on the ground
The petals are like a sun
On the top of the shoot's face.

*Amber Grose (7)*
*Alverton CP School*

## THE BEAUTIFUL SEED POEM

The seed is like a brown drum kit
Because of the colour
The roots are like sticks
Falling off the trees
The shoot is like a pencil
Long and green
The leaves are like green pieces of paper
Fluttering in the wind
The petals are like the wings of a bird
Dancing in the air.

*Harry Griffiths (7)*
*Alverton CP School*

## THE DAISY

The seed is like a sharp knife
Cutting through the soil
The roots are like a curling stick
Like a straw
The shoot is like an umbrella
Ready to open up
The leaves are like a bow and arrow
With a pointed end
The petals are like the sun
A fiery ball of colour.

*Joshua Wallis (6)*
*Alverton CP School*

## THE FIELD

I left the classroom to go outside
The bitter green grass field
Girls and boys playing
The ball bounces away
Kicking and throwing
Playing near the hall
Goalpost wobbled with the wind
Getting stronger
Thinking it's a dream
Fascinating footballers
Scoring at every minute
Just can't stop looking
My mum just nudged me
Was that true?
*It was a dream!*

*Laura James  (10)*
*Alverton CP School*

## CYGNETS

Excited to ride on their mother's back
Happy to live in their new world.
Sweet, creamy brown feathers,
Saying goodbye only three
Months old!

*Alison Pring  (11)*
*Alverton CP School*

## YOU'RE NOT PLAYING WITH US

Every day I lean against the tree
I wish I was having fun
Nobody likes me, just ignoring
Whispering about me.

I feel sad, and bored, 'Why am I here?'
I say over and over again.
I want to go, go away from this place.
All I can hear is, 'You're not playing with us,
You're not playing with us. You're not playing with us!'

*'You're not playing with us!'*

**Luke Jefferies (11)**
**Alverton CP School**

## THE PLANT POEM

The seed is like a stone
So round and hard
The roots are like long white straws
Sucking up the water
The shoot is like a stick
So straight and tall
The leaves are like some tears
They are pointed
The petals are like a plane
They are thin.

**Holly Collins (6)**
**Alverton CP School**

## BROTHERS AND SISTERS

When me and my brother are together
We shout, we scream, we hate each other
But when my brother sleeps at Nan's
I sneak in his room and take his CD's
When he gets back he always finds out
So I sneak them back in and hide before he shouts
Other times he can be nice
Like when I'm ill
He carries my food, he puts the TV on, he cleans my room.
Brothers and sisters aren't that bad,
Don't leave us alone because we'll get mad
We'll shout, we'll kick, we'll scream
Because other times we just can't cope.

*Louise Pickhaver  (10)*
*Alverton CP School*


## THE SEED

The seed is like a ball, it is round
The roots are like long straws, they are very long
The shoot is like a tower growing, it is big.
The leaves are like little feet, they are a long round shape
The petals are like balloons, they are a long stretchy shape.

*James Turpin  (6)*
*Alverton CP School*

## GHOSTLY SPEED

A zooming speedboat
Like lightning across the ocean
Going at an amazing rate
All a blur in the distance
Making a trail of white foam
There is an unknown driver
At the wheel of the monster
Running across the sea.

A cliff oh no! The beast
It's soaring up
To the great wall of death
But wait where did it go?
Has it fallen down to the
Deep sea bed?
Nobody knows!

*Ben Osborne  (9)*
*Alverton CP School*

## THE SEED POEM

The seed is like a cannonball
Because it's round
The stem is like a piece of string
Because it is straight
The roots are like worms
Because they are wiggly
The petals are like an Indian's necklace
Because they are pretty.

*Lewis Hole  (6)*
*Alverton CP School*

## THE SEED POEM

The seed is like a tea leaf
Waiting to be heated
The roots are like a horse's tail
Long and brown
The shoot is like a rocket
Reaching for the moon
The leaves are like green umbrellas
Waiting for some rain
The petals are like treasure
When the box has been opened.

*Kelvin James  (7)*
*Alverton CP School*

## WHAT IS A PLANT LIKE

The seed is like a cannonball
Ready to explode
The roots are like curly worms
So thin and soft
The shoot is like a pointed nail
Looking for the sun
The leaves are like a curled up slithering snake
So thick and hard
The petals are like a glittering diamond
Shining so bright.

*Rebecca Brooks  (7)*
*Alverton CP School*

## THE MOON MONSTER

The moon monster is coming
Get out of his way
There's no one to save us
And he's coming this way.

The moon monster is coming
We're all going to die
There's no one to save us
I wish we could fly.

The moon monster is going
We're all safe again
Here's someone to save us.

*Oliver Whiting (10)*
*Alverton CP School*

## SHADOW

If you stand with your
Back to the shining sun
Look in front and watch
Your shadow will dance and run.

Now stand in front of
The shining sun
Look in front your
Shadow's gone.

*Matthew Lodey (9)*
*Alverton CP School*

## KITTENS

Kittens, kittens
Prowling along the floor.

Jumping and scratching
Crawling up the curtains.

All day long you have so much fun
Until it's bedtime.

Purring, purring,
I want to come in.

A new day has begun
New laughter and fun!

*Lucy Frost (11)*
*Alverton CP School*

## CARING

C are for me
A nd I will care for you,
R eaching out to care for others
I s something everyone should do,
N ice people who care for others
G et lots of care back.

*Verity Stephan (11)*
*Alverton CP School*

## CAT'S EYES

Cat's eyes brightly glare at me,
From in the hedge and up the tree,
I get frightened when I see,
The creepy cats' eyes stare at me.
Then I wake up in my bed,
I find I'm safe and sound again,
I see my cat and hear the purr,
Then I smooth her tabby fur.
Then I look out into the night,
The sky is black and the moon is bright.
What's that down there on the grass?
Two cat's eyes like bright green glass.

*Natalie Richardson  (10)*
*Bodriggy Primary School*


## THE TIGER

The sky is a tiger,
When it slams its paws,
The lightning strikes with it.
When it goes to bed,
The hail drops dead!
When it's hungry,
The storm begins.
When it shakes,
The showers break   .
Tiger's angry loud he roars,
Thunder joins in and shakes the floor.

*Hannah Saunders  (9)*
*Bodriggy Primary School*

## THE WEATHER ANIMALS

The cloud is a horse
Rushing through the sky racing like it's never ran before.
The lightning hoof hits the church steeple
Down it tumbles.
The horse's hair wisps through leaves.
The horse's breath hustles through trees.
Suddenly the horse comes to a halt
It is no longer winter, spring has come.

The sun is a dragon breathing fiery fire
Burning down trees.
Its face shining in the sky.
Its tail hits roofs of houses.

The rain is a cat,
Milk dripping on the earth.
Its legs walking sneaking through the streets
Spitting on sight of a mouse person.

*Jenny Dawn Ritchie  (10)*
*Bodriggy Primary School*


## THE TIGER

The wind is a hungry tiger
Pouncing on houses and roaring
You walk away but it follows you everywhere
It won't go away
Its paw is the rain
Grabbing you but you run like a cheetah!
You get in but the tiger is still there.

*Hannah Smith  (10)*
*Bodriggy Primary School*

# ME

My mum likes doing sewing
My dad is going bald,
My uncle's very large
And also very old.

My sister likes her teddy
Grandad's drinking beer,
Auntie's out on holiday
Gran fell off the pier.

But I'm me
And that's final,
Nothing can change that
Or can it?

*Christopher Williams (10)*
*Bodriggy Primary School*


# BUBBLES

Big bubbles
Small bubbles
Yellow bubbles
White.

Soft bubbles
Green bubbles
All of them are light.

Bubbles can be stripy
Bubbles can be wet
Bubbles can be seen through
But they just can't be kept!

*Jason Sparks (8)*
*Bodriggy Primary School*

## THE WOLF WIND

The wind is a ferocious wolf hunting for a victim,
Its nippy, cold claws kills the sweltering heat.
Everything in its path shivers with fear,
The fear of going up, up and away.
It's looking for a way in,
Looking, looking.
It's found a way in!
The howl echoes through the house,
Your smell of fear gushes up its nostrils
It knows you're there . . .
Gently it glides up the stairs.
You can feel its cold breath on the back of your neck . . .

*Daniel Orchard  (10)*
*Bodriggy Primary School*

## BUBBLES

Bubbles are big and small
Bubbles can be long and tall.

Bubbles have lots of colours
Blow them fast there'll be others.

Bubbles is my favourite game
I try and give them all a name.

Bubbles in my bath are lots
Bubbles in the sink to clean pots.

*Amy Ellis  (8)*
*Bodriggy Primary School*

# BUBBLES

Big, small, fat, round,
Bubbles are quiet and don't make a sound,
Take your wand and watch them fly,
Watch them float into the sky.

Blue, green, yellow, pink,
If you look closely you'll see them link,
They look like a rainbow,
Made of soap,
They won't get annoying,
I'm sure you can cope.

It's nice in sunny weather,
To have bubbles as light as a feather,
Wave hello!
Wave goodbye!
Look at them - they can fly.

*Corinne Homer (8)*
*Bodriggy Primary School*


# BUBBLES

Bubbles are wet and round
When you burst them they do not make a sound
When you blow bubbles into the sky
You cannot see the colours because they are up so high
Bubbles are round, bouncy and colourful
Bubbles are beautiful things too.

*Craig Rennard (9)*
*Bodriggy Primary School*

## SPRING

Winter's past, spring is here
The air is fresh at the start of this new day
While the golden sun shines,
Swans swim on the crystal lake.
Streams are flowing bright, bright blue
And we are splashing in them!
Daffodils are growing along the hedgerows
As the butterflies flit all around us.
Newly born lambs and foals play in the fields
Watched by their mums.
How I love the new fresh smell of spring.

*Kerenza Berry (8)*
*Bodriggy Primary School*


## WINTER THOUGHTS

In winter the days are short
I lik e to throw snowballs
There are snowflakes and there are hailstones
I wear gloves and a scarf in the snow
The water in the pond was frozen
I had to break the ice so the fish could breathe
Some animals hibernate in winter, like the hedgehog
Some birds fly away to a warmer country.

*Chloe Amber Frost (7)*
*Bodriggy Primary School*

## FORMULA 1

Brightly coloured cars.
Spectators waiting for the start.
There they go!
Vroom, fast and noisy.
Tyres screeching around the corners.
People cheering, excited and happy.
'Come on, come on,' they shout.
Then out goes the chequered flag
The end of the race.

*Benjamin Peters (6)*
*Bodriggy Primary School*

## WEATHER POEM

Thundering skies a strong windy breeze
Hyper-hurricane's spinning around
Heavy rain shooting down
Sharp lightning firing down with an almighty crash.
Trees pulled out by their roots
Haystacks, bins and roof tiles all flying around
Telegraph poles in the middle of the road
Hailstones spitting down
And dark clouds covering the moon.

*Max Bell (11)*
*Bodriggy Primary School*

## UNTITLED

Shut up
Let's run
Let's hide
Let's have fun
Let's play a game
Oh stop hurting me
Stop it.
Oh there's the whistle
Oh well
Playtime's over.

*Samuel McBride (7)*
*Bodriggy Primary School*


## UNTITLED

At the bottom of the garden is a gate
Daddy made from a crate
Beyond the gate lies a lake
Where I go to meet my mate for a date
We catch the bus without any fuss
And go to the town for a skate.

*Colette Hawker*
*Bodriggy Primary School*

## WINTER THOUGHTS

Winter means curling up in a chair
And wearing warm jumpers.
I don't want to go outside.
It's warm inside.
Winter gives colds
And big thick blankets of snow.

*Scott Gunn (7)*
*Bodriggy Primary School*


## ABOUT FALMOUTH

People talking all the time
Dogs barking as though there was a crime.

People are boating
Feathers are floating.

Children are playing on the beach
In the water out of reach.

*Nicholas Hort (8)*
*Boskenwyn CP School*


## HARVEST TIME

The golden corn swaying
Swaying in the blowing wind
The sun is getting weaker
The corn looks like a running fox
Farmers cutting the fresh yellow corn
Storing it safely in the barn.

*Katie Pedley (8)*
*Boskenwyn CP School*

## THE MOUSEHOLE CAT

On the south coast of England,
In a cottage near the sea,
There lived a cat called Mowzer,
Who enjoyed fish for tea;

One dark and stormy evening,
There appeared a fearsome sight,
So Tom the brave old fisherman,
Went out into the night;

He threw out his fishing nets,
And caught a shoal of fish,
He escaped the angry storm cat,
And filled up every dish.

*Alexander Hort  (10)*
*Boskenwyn CP School*


## AT THE SEASIDE

Nippy breezes catching you as they go by,
Seagulls stand in position ready to fly.

Boats gently rocking from side to side,
Fifty pence a ticket if you want a ride.

People rushing by, never time to say hello
Fishermen say good day, their voices really bellow.

Shops packed like tinned sardines,
No one knows what 'Be quiet' means.

Now we have played on the beach, it's time to go home,
The beach is all quiet, sad and alone.

*Jinny Wadsworth  (10)*
*Boskenwyn CP School*

## MOUSEHOLE

Blue green sea wrinkling round boats,
Boats on ropes like dogs on leads.
Salty, sandy, slippy sand, more golden than gold,
Smelly sea water like fish and chips,
Air feeling like slippy smooth silk.
Rough hard buildings like concrete
Bendy houses along Celtic roads.

*Aine Bailey  (8)*
*Boskenwyn CP School*


## FISHES

A fish is a frigate that roams the sea.
He speeds around, his energy never goes down.
He conquered the conger, killed the krill.
The fish is the emperor of the sea.

*Julio Birch  (11)*
*Boskenwyn CP School*


## MOUSEHOLE

Water flat as a pancake,
Water running onto the rough stones,
Stones rough as sandpaper.
Smell of fish and chips
Making your mouth water.

*Louise Williams  (9)*
*Boskenwyn CP School*

## MOUSEHOLE

Fishing boats go out the teeny, tiny Mousehole,
Busy shops in the town,
Noisy cars drive quickly past the beach.
The smell of beer coming from the pubs.
Boats look like they're dancing slowly.
The air feels like a cold hairdryer,
The smell of seaweed from the sea,
Quiet narrow dark alleys are all around,
Bumpy, white walls on houses.

*Simoné Foreman  (10)*
*Boskenwyn CP School*


## THE BEACH

The blue waves crashing against the jagged cliffs,
Silky sand shining in the bright sunset,
Wind curling around the rough cliff faces.
The sun beating down on the sparkling water,
The booming sea rising, rising
Small damp caves embedded in the cliffs,
Children playing in the silky sand.

*Peter Symms  (11)*
*Boskenwyn CP School*


## FEELINGS

Happy and joyful
My friends called for me to play
It's fun to have friends.

*Catherine Mutton  (10)*
*Callington CP School*

## FEELINGS

I feel dead so I'll have a bit of bread,
It feels rough and a bit duff!
I feel sad but I'm mad!
I'm crazy and a bit dazy!
I feel blind and a bit kind.
I feel ill so I'll have a pill!
I'm wheezy and it's breezy.

*Louise Hatton (10)*
*Callington CP School*


## FEELINGS

Felt cold, all alone.
The wind blows my feelings drop.
Then the sun rises.

*Karl Langman (11)*
*Callington CP School*


## MY FEELINGS

My feelings are bright,
As I dream all day and night.
And I feel so well.

*Steven Pound (10)*
*Callington CP School*

## FEELINGS

F urious is what I feel,
E verybody has to know,
E ven people it doesn't concern.
L ight-hearted me is completely different,
I  want to sing and dance and play,
N o one has to feel unhappy,
G lad me is different again.

*Kathryn Skelton  (11)*
*Callington CP School*


## FEELINGS

There was a mean old man from Taiwan,
Who decided to make a huge plan,
To fill the whole world,
Full of hatred not love.
That mean old man from Taiwan.

*Cara Bowers  (11)*
*Callington CP School*


## FUNNY FEELINGS

There was a young man from Darjeeling,
Who couldn't control his feelings,
One moment he was glad,
Then suddenly got so mad,
That he stood up and shot through the ceiling.

*Rebecca Leverington  (11)*
*Callington CP School*

## HOW I FEEL - I'M NOT SURE

I feel happy
I feel sad
I get mad
When I am sad.

When I am bored
I am tired
I am grumpy
When I am scared.

It makes me angry
When I am not sure!

*Philip Stephens  (10)*
*Callington CP School*

## FEELINGS

F   eelings can be sad.
E   asily bad.
E   nd never. Always together.
L   aughter, tears, love nowhere.
I   'm sad all day.
N   othing keeps me away.
G   oing through the day.
S   ad and low. Happy no.

*Sarah Moir  (11)*
*Callington CP School*

## FEELINGS

Sometimes we feel happy
As joyful as can be
You dance around and play all day
Oh so lovely it is to be glee!

Sometimes we feel angry
We shout and scream at the top of our voice!
With rage and fury
We kick and thump and land on the floor with a bump.

Sometimes we feel calm and peaceful
Lying in bed we are asleep, we dream
Of stars and moons
In peaceful slumber deep.

*Kayleigh Wheatley (10)*
*Callington CP School*


## FEELINGS

F   eeling is great
E   xcitement is too
E   very Friday I feel like air
L   iving in the breeze
I   n summer and in winter
N   othing seems alive
G   liding in the air
S   liding in through the clouds.

*Jade Turner (11)*
*Callington CP School*

## FEELINGS

Feelings come straight from the heart
Feelings can be hurt
But feelings can also feel good
Sometimes it feels like you don't have feeling.

Feelings can be hurt
Lots of feelings are for different reasons
Sometimes you feel like you don't have any reasons
You can have feelings like angry and upset.

Lots of feelings are for different reasons
But feelings can also feel good
You can have feelings like angry and upset
Feelings come straight from the heart.

*Samantha Biggs  (11)*
*Callington CP School*


## FEELINGS

F  riends are fun to play with
E  xcitement comes with them.
E  very Friday of a week tiredness comes
L  ying in bed not wanting to get up
I   nside at times we feel let down
N  ever knowing what's going to happen next
G  etting started in the morning is always an effort
S  unday's the end of the week
          Another week starting tomorrow.

*Katie Williams  (10)*
*Callington CP School*

## HOW I FEEL

I like to laugh,
I like to run,
I like to dance under the sun,
But now all is done,
I want to do something new,
Something I've never done before,
Maybe fly up in the sky,
Or live under the sea for history,
But all is well,
I'll think of something somehow,
I like to laugh,
I like to run,
I like to dance under the sun.

*Lea-Anne Ansell  (11)*
*Callington CP School*


## AS I WAS WALKING DOWN THE ROAD

As I was walking down the road
I came across a watery toad.
Now I'd seen toad in a book
So I stopped to take a closer look.
But along came a car and that was that
Because one hop later the toad went splat!

*Adam Holloway  (11)*
*Callington CP School*

## MY FEELINGS

You wake up the sun is shining
Joyfully, gleefully happy not sad.
The sun is shining, bright and sparkling.

You wake up the sun has gone away
But now just darkness and rain
Lashing from the sky
You're sad and gloomy.

You wake up. What's this?
Snow! Snowmen, snowballs
Giggling and laughing
You're better now.

*Serena Skews  (10)*
*Callington CP School*


## NIGHTMARE

I wake up in the night,
Then freeze with fear.
Darkness closes in,
Scared in the night.
Is there someone outside?
Does fate draw near?
I can't stand any more,
Reach for the light,
And all ends in a flash!

*Kathy Mackrory  (11)*
*Callington CP School*

# THE MAGIC BOX

I will put in the box
the day the huge world began,
the day the magnificent computer was born,
the special moment I saw my parents.

I will put in the box
the great sadness when Princess Diana died,
the happiness she brought to the whole world,
my first day at school.

I will put in the box
the wildest hurricane ever recorded,
the first snowflake that fell on the earth,
the exciting test flight of a Boeing 747.

I will put in the box
the last word of an age-old uncle,
a giant tidal wave from a Caribbean beach,
the leap of a hungry ferocious Piranha.

My box is made from brightly glowing laser beams,
with a wild face on the lid,
its hinges are fingers from a dead Aborigine.

I will rollerblade in my box
bravely on the biggest Half Pipe in the world
then I shall claim a magnificent trophy
for my daring record attempt.

*Tom West (10)*
*Camborne St Meriadoc CE Junior School*

# THE MAGIC BOX

I will put in the box
the roar of the ocean waves on a shingle beach,
the mystery of the universe in all its glory,
the beautiful sight of the Aurora Borealis on a cold, starry night.

I will put in the box
the soundless flight of an owl,
cubes of ice from the mountain of Kilimanjaro,
a rock from the deepest ravine floor.

I will put in the box
the white sky and blue clouds of the Fifth Dimension,
the last words of a very old man,
and the first patter of tiny feet.

I will put in the box
the many names of God,
a little robin with a headache,
and a person with sore wings.

My box is crafted from books that I've read,
it is lined with the world's finest silks,
the lock is made from ivory,
and the key is made of gold.

I shall rollerblade in my box,
on the flat tarmac expanses of San Francisco,
then I'll stop at the Golden Gate Bridge
and watch the water go by.

*Jake Smith  (11)*
*Camborne St Meriadoc CE Junior School*

## THE EVENING MAGIC

An old crane rusting sadly on the quay,
A beautiful ship silhouetted in a muddy dry dock,
The treetops echo with bird songs,
Crooked trees stand bent and knobbly,
Hang over the path as I run,
Stones sharp as daggers beneath my feet,
I stop to see the clouds move
Higher than the treetops,
Lower than the blue.
A robin poses in a tree,
I hear a stream trickle on its journey,
As evening dawns in the afternoon sky,
A shiver runs through the reeds in the chilly wind,
As the river gently and majestically rolls by.

*Rebecca Williams  (10)*
*Calstock CP School*


## TREES

When I walk past trees in the summer
I think they're so pretty.
In the summer they shine in the light.
I like the autumn when I can jump on all the leaves.
In the winter the trees look so bare and cold
I want to take them inside with me.
But mum says they live outside
So I leave them alone.

*Robin Williams  (10)*
*Calstock CP School*

## THE ALIEN

As he creeps up behind me,
He taps me on the back,
They swarm around me,
What shall I do?

A shiver runs down my back,
He freezes me, I can't move,
My feet are stuck to the ground,
'Help me! Help me,' I scream.

They push me into their spaceship,
On their planet it's dead and cold,
I'll never get back. That's the end of me.
It's the *Alien!*

*Lamorna Elmer (9)*
*Calstock CP School*

## CHOCOLATE LEAVES IN AUTUMN

Chocolate-coloured leaves,
On the tree,
In autumn,
Nearly about to fall,
Then they sail to the ground.
On the ground they are crispy and brittle.
Like a golden stage.

*Samantha Davies (11)*
*Calstock CP School*

## THE WOODS

The knobbly trees stand high as if they were important.
The birds sleeping in their high-up nests.
Birds showing off their colours proudly.
Ivy berries tempting us to eat them.
The leaves crunching under our feet.
A hollow tree like a drum.
Shoots poking out of the ground everywhere
And jagged rocks sticking out of the path making me trip up.
The clouds in the sky looking like giant hovering spaceships.
Bare, cold, trees hanging over us.
Soft, furry moss covering the trees.
Vines hanging from the branches clinging on tight,
Holly leaves are prickly on the branches.
Walking by wearing out their path,
Going home to our warm, cosy homes.

*Amy Elmer (10)*
*Calstock CP School*


## COTEHELE QUAY

Flapping paper, golden reads
Stone buildings seem to shiver
My feet shiver in my shoes
As the river rolls on.

The crunching leaves and sprouting plants
As the branches spread like fingers
Old rotting tree stumps with moss
The dense undergrowth goes green
As spring arrives.

*Elizabeth Crowell (10)*
*Calstock CP School*

## THE ENCHANTED TREE

The summer trees stood like kings in the lush meadow,
The fresh green leaves mingled with the bronze as they began to take
                                        over the summer trees.
Hazel leaves swirled around a chestnut trunk.
The leaves glided down gracefully, curling as they landed on the
                                        forest floor.
Crisp leaves lay crackling on a soft bed of moss.
The colourful leaves swerve to the floor making a carpet of gold,
Blazing as if on fire.
The magical trees' branches stood silhouetted against the evening sky.

*Madeline Amy Spurr  (10)*
*Calstock CP School*

## SEASONS

Summer lush green,
Now becomes autumn,
Chocolate and hazel,
Magical maybe.
Leaves from trees,
Silently float,
To the ground,
Like a golden floor,
Crunchy fire,
Burn the leaves,
For winter.

*Joanna Smith  (10)*
*Calstock CP School*

## THE ALIEN

Smoking
face in the darkness
a luminous green
face, purple eyes
in the darkness staring
watching my every move
all you see are
purple eyes and a
red light
glowing
in the dark
Alien
smoke
in the
air polluting
the world's
atmosphere.

*Harry Barnett (10)*
*Calstock CP School*


## NOVEMBER

No flowers blooming in colourful bunches.
No salads fresh and crunchy.
No sunny days so hot and dry.
No tweeting birds so nice and happy.
No swimming in the cool gentle sea.

*Rachael Shayer (11)*
*Calstock CP School*

46

## MY COLD POEM

My feet are like an ice pole, I can't move my toes
My lips are as cold as a freezer,
My fingers are as cold as a tree trunk.
Ducks are swimming in the freezing cold water,
The water is as cold as an ice cube,
The leaves are crunching as I walk through them all,
I feel like a frozen sheep in the field,
I am so cold and no one takes any notice of me.

*Leigh-Anne Alford (10)*
*Calstock CP School*


## THE COLD

I am writing
With my cold numb hands
That feel like icicles
I am unable to write properly
My ears feel like they're made of ice
And about to fall off my head.

*Kai Kenyon (10)*
*Calstock CP School*


## WINTER IS COMING

The large majestic trees
Green, lush and beautiful
Slowly changing colours
Brick bronze and brown
Silently fall to the ground
A crispy, crunchy, crackling sound.

*William Shayer (10)*
*Calstock CP School*

## NOVEMBER

No sticky ice-cream melting in the sun,
No sunbathing on a hot golden beach.
No baby birds chirping for their food.
No swimming in the cool wavy water.
No crunchy red and green salads.
No blue skies with white, fluffy clouds.
No beautiful flowers showing off their colours.

*Laurie Mason Kaye (10)*
*Calstock CP School*


## THE LOG

The log is lumpy and smooth
Sometimes curly
Little creatures make holes in it
It smells as though it has been burnt
It looks like a skeleton.

*Micayla Barnet (8)*
*Calstock CP School*


## A HOLIDAY

H  is for holiday, here at last.
O  is for orange, we are eating on the beach.
L  is for lolly, that I bought in the town.
I  is for injury, I fell on the sand.
D  is for days, they do go quick.
A  is for another ice-cream please.
Y  is for yellow, the sun's in the sky.

*Emma Clay (9)*
*Calstock CP School*

## MY AUTUMN TREE

A magical tree with beautiful colours,
Chestnut, yellow and dark red.
Reflecting in the sun
Slowly gliding and swerving down,
It looks like a carpet on the ground.
When I step on the leaves,
It is crisp and crunchy
Under my feet
And all around.

*Matthew Wilson  (10)*
*Calstock CP School*


## MY HERO

A hero is brave and strong.
A hero is a very good fighter.
A hero is good at killing people.
A hero is nice to his friends.
My hero is James Bond.

*James Vaughan  (9)*
*Calstock CP School*


## SANTA

When I go to bed at night
I cuddle teddy really tight.
On Christmas Eve when Santa's here
When the bells ring you must not fear.
For he is here to bring to me
A present to put under the Christmas tree.

*Stephanie Hobbs  (9)*
*Calstock CP School*

## THE LOST KEY

Where is the key?
Nobody knows.
Where to look?
Nobody knows.
At the back of the school through a gate.
Old and grassy brown and knobbly.
Under a tree stump and the mud
Will be the key you are looking for.

*Emma Price (9)*
*Calstock CP School*


## DAVE

Dave was a slave
Who would not shave,
Dave stayed in a cave ,
That looked like a grave,
Dave is brave!

*Vanessa Hemmett (9)*
*Calstock CP School*


## THE KEY

The key was hidden a long time ago.
I wonder where it is?
Nobody knows where to look.
Look for the water that goes round and round.
Look up where the water comes down, down, down.

*Now it is found!*

*Laura Stephens (9)*
*Calstock CP School*

## THE MAGIC TREE

Where is the key?
Where can it be?
Please find the key.
The door needs you and me
To free the magic tree.
The lock is by your knee
Please find the key.
To free the magic tree.

*Alexandra Allden (8)*
*Calstock CP School*


## HOLIDAY

H   is for holiday, here at last.
O   is for oysters, in rock pools.
L   is for lovely, a beautiful view.
I    is for ice, that is in orange juice.
D   is for dinner, having it on the beach.
A   is for apples, eating on the sand.
Y   is for yacht, sailing on the sea.

*Rachel Fowler (10)*
*Calstock CP School*


## UNTITLED

Parts of the brown muddy waves
Sparkling in the sun
Boat bobbing up and down
Ducks splashing having fun.

*Christopher Crowell (8)*
*Calstock CP School*

## HOLIDAYS

H   is for holiday, we're having bad weather.
O   is for orange, juicy and sweet.
L   is for lolly, sticky but delicious.
I    is for ice, freezing cold.
D   is for dancing, to the music
A   is for apple, crunch, crunch.
Y   is for yawning, tired and sleepy.
S   is for sleeping, fast asleep.

*Christopher Nance  (9)*
*Calstock CP School*


## THE BOBBING BUOYS

Bobbing buoys across the river
Up and down it doesn't matter.
Ducks in the water
Ducks swimming round.
The viaduct's shadow glows in the sun.
Water is cold
Water is browny-green.
The reeds swish and swosh
And make the strangest sounds.

*Francesca Hannon  (8)*
*Calstock CP School*

# THE DOG

There was once a dog called Suzie
Where did she come from? Nobody knows!
Where was she born? Nobody knows!
What was her name? Nobody knows!
Did she like playing? Nobody knows!
How many feet did she have? Nobody knows!
Did she like children? Nobody knows!

*Kevin Pethick (9)*
*Calstock CP School*


# FUNFAIR

I'm going to the funfair,
Lots of rides to enjoy.
Big wheels and all.
Doughnuts, candy and fizzy drinks.
Lots of people big and small.
I'm not going home!

*Sam Leonard Williams (9)*
*Calstock CP School*


# THE RIVER

The river rippling cold and freezing.
The wind howling
The rain dripping
The waves crashing and bashing
The buoys are bobbing as the boats go by.
The ducks swimming up and down.

*Kit Kaye (8)*
*Calstock CP School*

## JESUS THEY WILL CALL HIM

Joseph and Mary have a baby,
Jesus they will call him.
The baby gently clasps the straw,
Jesus they will call him.
The donkey all shaggy and brown,
Jesus they will call him,
Snoozes gently next to him.

*Clare Edmunds  (10)*
*Calstock CP School*


## MY FAMILY

Mum says
I am the muckiest,
I am the stickiest,
Joe is the trickiest.
Mum says
I am the dirtiest,
So she calls me Pong Wiff.

Mum says
Hannah is funnier than Joe,
I am calmer wherever I go.
Hannah is happier when she's with Timo.
But I say
Dad gets angry
So we call him Victor Meldrew.

*Charlotte Brand  (9)*
*Chacewater CP School*

## I'D RATHER BE

I'd rather be a chip than a fish/
I'd rather be ground than air.
I'd rather be thin than fat.
I'd rather be a dog than a cat.
I'd rather be a father than a mother.
I'd rather be a sister than a brother.
I'd rather be a runner than a thrower.
I'd rather be a gardener than a grower.
I'd rather be a mat than a rug.
I'd rather be digging than dug.
I'd rather be a pull than a tug.
I'd rather not be a thug.

*Ben Sowden (9)*
*Chacewater CP School*

## ACROSTIC POEM

D   rawing is what I like best although
R   eally my mum's better at
A   rt
W   orking with paint, pens and
I    nk
N   ext week I might finish my masterpiece
G   reat artists aren't told, 'Stop now!'

*Rory Dunham (9)*
*Chacewater CP School*

## SMUGGLING

Warm and snug in bed I lie,
I hear the hooves trot by,
I pull the covers about my head
And tightly shut my eyes.
Don't open the shutter
Just stay in bed,
Ignore this warning
By morning you're dead.

Has a ship been lured to the rocks,
All the sailors drowned?
Has a cart been loaded yet,
The precious cargo found?
Don't open the shutter
Just stay in bed,
Ignore this warning
By morning you're dead.

Barrels hidden in secret dens,
If you find them at play
Don't disturb the smuggler's hoard,
Leave well alone, just walk away.

*Sarah Lane  (8)*
*Chacewater CP School*


## I'D RATHER BE

I'd rather be a ping than a pong.
I'd rather be a ding than a dong.
I'd rather be a grandpa not a granny.
I'd rather be a giggle than a groan.
I'd rather be a laugh than a moan.

*Tanya Johns  (9)*
*Chacewater CP School*

## THE STONE CHURCH

The stone church stands cold,
It stands day and night for life,
Till the sun wakes up,
The cold night comes in to rest,
Before the birds start to sing.

*Sarah Brooks  (11)*
*Chacewater CP School*


## SILENCE

Frozen window pronounces in chronicles,
Statue stands stiffly silent,
Holy Bible rests privately,
Pillar stiffens mightily proud,
Beautiful arch gracefully watches,
While the frosty font sits watchfully.

*Lucy J Heffer  (10)*
*Chacewater CP School*


## CHURCH ON THE HILL

From the flickering candle
To the fantastically toned window.
From the lovely decorated hassocks
To the extremely important cross on the wall.
From the loud tall organ
To the small quiet piano.
From the unfeeling floor
To the flickering candle.

*Adalean Coade  (9)*
*Chacewater CP School*

## INSIDE THE CHURCH

From the ornate pulpit reflecting
To the varnished ark-like roof.

From the superior statue standing
To the dusty Bible watching.

From the antique table holding
To the pillowed pews praying.

From the rusty organ chanting
To the monstrous pillar stalking.

From the gleaming wine swirling strangely
To the ornate pulpit reflecting.

*Jordan Hamilton (10)*
*Chacewater CP School*

## CHURCH'S COMPONENTS

Musical piano curiously watches,
The melting candle flickers gracefully,
Filled pulpit stands proud,
The solid door mournfully swings,
The cross is breathless, it's hanging proudly,
Towering pillars patiently overlook,
Curved arches peacefully stand,
The candle burning, brightly blazes,
The solid piano peacefully playing.

*Christopher Turner (10)*
*Chacewater CP School*

## INSIDE THE CHURCH

Proud altar watches endlessly,
Frozen statue glares sightlessly,
The inflexible candle stands peacefully,
Powerful organ booms proudly,
Gigantic pillar towers triumphantly,
Marble pulpit waits patiently.

*Amy Jose  (11)*
*Chacewater CP School*


## CHACEWATER'S CHURCH

Great granite arches,
Strong pillars straining beneath
Sharing their great weight.

Strong pillars stand high,
Long candle burning bright,
Oak statue standing tall,
Long pews always creaking.

*David Tamblyn  (10)*
*Chacewater CP School*


## MY MUMMY

M   y mum is marvellous,
U   sually happy,
M   ainly laughing,
M   aking funny voices,
Y   ou would giggle!

*Alishea Buck  (8)*
*Chacewater CP School*

## SHIP IN A BOTTLE

The ship is a cat, trapped in a cage,
My mane is sticky with glue.
My proud head is now the carved bow,
My sea is a blue, still floor.
Lifeless.

Only adventures in my mind.
Storms are my tears.
My world is a transparent fish tank,
That's motionless.
My flags and sails are dead,
The cork comes out,
Life is breathed in.

Trapped in a bottle that's dead!

*Martha Whitfeld (8)*
*Chacewater CP School*


## THE SHIP IN THE BOTTLE

There was no action.
I float in a wax sea,
There are no fish in the sea,
And my world is white and lonely.
I sit in the window as the cars go by,
The dust settles on my bottle.
And our nets are cast out but
No fish come for us to take back to port.
No people will be there on land to cheer us.

*Alice Hunter (9)*
*Chacewater CP School*

## GAZING

From the translucent stained glass window
To the cold, unfeeling floor.

From the tunefully sounding organ
To the discreetly watching statue.

From the grand attentive altar
To the patiently waiting pews.

From the glowing, flickering candle
To the mighty marble pulpit.

From the ornate sandstone font
To the story-telling windows.

From the groaning supportive pillars
To the imposing silent arches.

From the arched magnificent roof
To the unnoticed humble chairs.

From the translucent stained glass windows
To the cold, unfeeling floor.

*Victoria Ball  (11)*
*Chacewater CP School*


## RULES

R  ules are necessary in life.
U  nruly behaviour is wrong.
L  earn rules of the road.
E  veryone should live by rules.
S  ome people break rules.

*Richard Dickman  (10)*
*Crowan CP School*

## SILENCE

Silence is when you can hear things, listen,
When the bird spoons and glides down to the ground.
Silence is when the mouse gasps for breath,
Staring at the crumbs on the table and on the floor,
And the cat on my lap ready to pounce any second.
Silence is when you can hear things, listen,
When my pen leaks over the end of the table.
Silence is when a man looks out through his soaked coat
At the end of the pier at the water trying to throw itself onto the pier.
Silence is when you can hear things, listen . . .

*Christopher Smith  (9)*
*Crowan CP School*


## DARK

The moon is burning in the sky,
Like the sun.
Lightning strikes.
The clouds cover the sky.
The rain smacks my window.
The wind howls like a wolf.
The lightning strikes the wires
And falls in a flame.
As I sit there looking around in bed,
The clouds uncover the moon.
The lightning stops
And I go to sleep.

*Tom Berryman  (9)*
*Crowan CP School*

## THE STORM

The storm, brave and grey.
As quick as lightning.
As sly as a fox.
The fangs bite away.
Vicious and fierce,
Comes in packs from everywhere.

*Christopher Green (11)*
*Crowan CP School*


## DARKNESS IS

Darkness is disgusting,
When you can't see
Who or what
You are stepping on.
It could be a bug
And lots of little slugs!

*David Newbery (10)*
*Crowan CP School*


## STORM

The storm sprints through the air.
It springs at you.
Its big, strong paws claw at the earth.
Its fierce mouth echoes out loud, roaring like thunder.
The eyes flash like lightning.
Its wild tail pushes wind
From side to side.

*Paul Douglass (10)*
*Crowan CP School*

## SILENCE

Silence is when you can hear things,
Listen,
Silence is loneliness,
Sitting on your own,
Quiet, nothing.
Darkness creeps over you,
Like a shadow,
Watching, stepping,
I, 2, 3,
Silence is when you can hear things,
Listen . . .

*Jenny Rowe  (10)*
*Crowan CP School*


## THE STORM CAT

The storm cat prowls around the city,
leaps, crashes, it hits the road, knocks down the tower
with one great paw.
Picks up trees and cars and hurls them into houses.
Chases the sea onto the cliffs and the bay,
flooding houses and halls.
Reports coming in from all over England as the
storm cat is still raging on its quest to destroy the city.
Fire crews fight for people's lives.
But now the storm cat is tired, he backs away and runs.
He cannot be stopped.

*Chris Butcher  (10)*
*Crowan CP School*

## DARKNESS

Dark is a scary feature,
In the dark you get a scary creature.
You don't know what's round the door.
There's a squeaky sound,
Look there, look what I've found!
I'll go to bed,
Up my ladder,
Going up, is that an adder?
No, it's just my watch in the corner.
Hear a crash and a smash,
Go out of the door,
Down the hall,
In the kitchen, kick a ball,
Something's running,
Coming, quick,
Coming in a tick . . .
It's only my dog.
I walk in through the porch,
My torch fades away,
Clock strikes twelve, it's
Another day.

*Anthony White  (10)*
*Crowan CP School*


## THE STORM

The storm, hissing and wailing under the door.
Spitting and scratching outside in the dark.
An angry, playful push rattles the letterbox.
Paws and claws patting and trampling along the floors.

*Michelle Townsend  (10)*
*Crowan CP School*

## WHAT'S THAT NOISE?

What's that noise?
It's just the wind
Rattling the window.
What's that noise?
It's just the creak when Dad
Walks over the floorboards.

What's that noise?
It's just one of your teddy bears
Falling off your shelf.
What's that noise?
It's just the tap dripping.

What's that noise?
I don't know!

*Tamsyn Jones (9)*
*Crowan CP School*


## SILENCE

Silence is when you can hear things.
Listen. I can hear some water,
Trickling down the stream.
I can hear a blackbird,
Singing in the tree.

I can hear the birds,
Rustling for their grub.
I can hear some stamping,
Hard on the ground.
I can hear some stamping,
Never to be found.

*Nicholas Humphrey (10)*
*Crowan CP School*

## JULY

Days in July are always hot,
Outdoor swimming days,
Days in July are always hot,
Play in the garden,
Days in July are always hot,
Time for lunch, a salad,
Days in July are always hot,
Having so much fun,
Days in July are always hot,
It's over, I have to go to bed,
Days in July are always hot,
It's so light,
Days in July are always hot,
Tomorrow will come,
Fun will start again,
Days in July are always hot.

*Rosie Williams (9)*
*Crowan CP School*


## STORM

Storm, wings of cloud, voice of thunder,
Breath of lightning,
Tail of a tornado.
Its claws rip the tiles off roofs,
Causing flooding and havoc,
With an eye for flesh.
The creator of death, terror hissing
Through the sky,
Hovering smoke whirling about it.
Sharp, cold, grey. Prowling the
Night sky without warning.

*Abigail Norcross (10)*
*Crowan CP School*

## WHAT'S THAT CREAKING ON THE STAIR?

What's that creaking on the stair?
It's a tremacrog on that stair
Creeping quietly with long, sharp teeth,
Waiting there for someone to go downstairs,
Then he'll gobble them up
And keep on waiting there.

What's that gurgling over my bed?
It's a gurglevem waiting for me to go to sleep,
Then he'll drop down and eat me up,
With pointed spikes,
Then he'll climb back up
And go to his slimy bed.

What's that glowing over there?
It's a truglegrin with glowing eyes
And warm and sour breath,
Breathing only when I do,
He's waiting till the gurglevem eats me,
Then he'll feast on my bones.

What's that light over there?
It's a vamslime waiting to grab me,
The tremacrog's coming too near,
The gurglevem's gurgling louder,
The truglegrin's eyes are glowing brighter,
Then suddenly,
A very bright light comes into my room,
*Aaargh!*

It's only my pussy cat,
Coming to keep
All those nasties away.

*Trystan Spalding-Jenkin (9)*
*Crowan CP School*

## STORM NIGHT

Outside a storm is raging,
The night outside is wild.
Crashing, smashing trees together.
The moon is disappearing into the night.
Claps of thunder out in the dark.
Dogs are barking.
I can smell burning.
My mum lights a candle.
The power has gone out.
I can see the candle giving a single light.
We are waiting for the night to go.
The night is going slowly.
Giving way for morning.

*James Fletcher*
*Crowan CP School*


## SILENCE

Silence is when you can hear things, listen,
hear the rattle of the classroom drawers,
hear the mouse scuttle along the floors.
Silence is when you can hear things, listen,
hear the trees shake and sway,
hear the wind blow rubbish away.
Silence is when you can hear things, listen,
hear the people kicking the ball around,
hear people falling head-first on the ground.
Silence is when you can hear things, listen,
hear the teachers start to shout,
hear the birdies fly about.
Silence is when you can hear things, listen.

*Stuart Gaston  (10)*
*Crowan CP School*

## THE NIGHTMARE

The dark, black figure
moves silently towards me,
a silhouette against the
moonlit sky.

The murky trees sway in
the cold wind
and skeletons creep out
of their graves into the
world they once lived in.

Owls hoot in the
whispering trees,
the shadowy figure
commences slowly towards me,
his hands reach out to
grab me.

And then I wake up,
switch on the light,
breathe a sigh of relief,
the darkness has gone.

*Amy Hall  (10)*
*Crowan CP School*

## THE STORM

The nasty storm
Spits wind and fire,
Black and ugly,
Roaring through the night.

*Nicky Turner  (11)*
*Crowan CP School*

## SILENCE IS . . .

Silence
is when I hear things.
Listen, spiders scatter across my page.
Listen, pen leaks along my table.
Listen . . .
knobs in my head rattle.
Listen . . .
footsteps come.
Listen, clouds move across the light blue sky.
Listen . . .
caterpillar walks along a green leaf in the tree.
Listen . . .

*Catherine Payne  (11)*
*Crowan CP School*


## SILENCE

Silence is when you can hear things
Listen . . .
I can hear the brains thinking,
I can hear pencils writing,
I can hear bees humming,
I can hear the class next door mumbling.
Ssh! I can hear something . . .
I can hear a rubber, rubbing out,
I can hear cars go past the school,
I can hear ants walking across the ground,
I can hear caterpillars crunching leaves.
Listen, I can hear . . .

*Alexandra Durham  (10)*
*Crowan CP School*

## SILENCE

Silence is when you can hear things,
Listen
As the pen writes in silence,
And a cow walks to the hay.
Silence is teeth screeching inside your head,
Over and over again.
Silence is taking off a top of a pen and
shuffling back into your chair.
Silence is someone turning a page,
A screeching noise.
Silence is a rustle of trees swaying in the wind.
Silence is someone thinking and
Rumbles like a bee's wings.
Silence is chalk writing with a squeak.
Silence is a butterfly breathing.
Silence is strange!

*Jake Hawkey (9)*
*Crowan CP School*


## SILENCE

Silence is where you can hear things,
Listen.
Pens scribbling on the desk.
Computers humming out of action.
Bushes rumbling and the wind howling.
Busy people out shopping and drinking.
Teachers making the chalk scream.

*Leanne Warrick (10)*
*Crowan CP School*

## DARKNESS IN MY BEDROOM

Folded clothes look like monsters,
Glowing teddy's eyes staring at me,
White seashells dancing
To the rhythm of the night.

A thumping drumming bang,
Dogs, bad dream or
Footsteps on the stairs?

Damp, musty blackness
Falling down on me.

*Emma Rosevear  (11)*
*Crowan CP School*

## SIMILES

As unfunny as the girl near the end of our table.
As dead as choccy (very tasty)!
As unhappy as the person I stamped on in a footie match.
As silly as a nutty clown.
As weird as my brother.
As horrible as homework.
As confused as me at school!

*James Smith  (11)*
*Crowan CP School*

## THE STORM

The storm
With its killing claws.
Hear a crash in the darkness,
Hear a growling noise.

*Sharon Tanner (11)*
*Crowan CP School*


## IT

It had a fiery crest and a sharp pointed beak,
Long stalking legs and terrible claws,
A golden shape with glinting eyes,
It stood there, staring at me.

I turned away, started to run,
But that golden shape came after me,
I couldn't look back, my heart was pounding,
Those terrible claws I saw up above.

The thing closed in, gliding high,
Ruffling feathers and wings widespread,
It swooped down, grabbed hold of me,
Then up, up, up, it soared away.

The thing seemed to hover above the sea,
Then down, down, down it went,
A patch of land appeared from nowhere,
What was it, where were we?

*Tristan Tremain (10)*
*Launceston CP School*

## MARTIAL EAGLE

Arising up with powerful wings.
Swirling as it's airborne.
The graceful speed.
Soaring with catching feet.
Grasping at its prey.
The winds dance.
Furiously energetically.
Swooping rapidly.
The swift motion.
Moving side to side.
Roaring in pain.
Expiring with its last breath.

*Neil Glover  (11)*
*Launceston CP School*


## EAGLE

A silent predator,
Looking for prey,
Flying in the moonlight,
Feathers gleaming,
Claws razor sharp,
Quick to catch its targeted prey.
Flying high, his eyesight is keen,
His sharp eyes sight a mouse,
He claws his target,
And selfishly eats with no disturbance.
High in the tree the prey's blood drips.
Deadly in the moonlight he glides,
Ready to pounce again.

*Mark Downing  (11)*
*Launceston CP School*

## THE CALF

Out on the rocky plains of the moor,
Where the big hills rest as they erode away,
Lies a shed.
Inside is a cow hiding a secret.

Then suddenly a small weak calf appears,
He looks cautiously around.
Breathing his first spluttering breaths,
He walks to his mother, shaking as he goes.

He starts suckling as the delighted mother licks him.
The wind scares her calf,
She comforts him.
Then he settles down to rest again.

*Jeremy Cole (10)*
*Launceston CP School*


## A WINDY DAY

Movement is in the air,
All around us we can feel it,
And look up at the sky on a wonderful day.

The sky is full of movement,
The sun around the clouds,
Now the wind is getting tougher.

A gale blows in from the north,
And whips down trees and telephone wires.
Hedges blow down,
The gale rages past.
We run for our houses and warm up
By the fire.

*Scott Baker (10)*
*Launceston CP School*

## THE WEATHER DAY

Snowy mist surrounding the road,
The sun on its way to push the mist away.
The mist as grey as a rock,
The sun brighter than diamond,
Rising till it stops.

The mist going away
It will not come again
Till the next weather day.
The rain trying to fight the sun.
The clouds are grumpy,
They let out a shine, reds, blues, greens, fighting the sun,
The sun and the rains are gone with the rainbow.

The sun is afraid,
It hides behind the clouds,
The cream-white clouds protect the sun.

*Christopher Mooney (10)*
*Launceston CP School*


## MY CAT TABBY

I have a cat called Tabby,
He's a very cuddly cat.
He roams around the garden all day,
And curls up to me at night.
He plays with his brother all the time
And beats him at a game of catch.
He has a habit of waking you up in the morning,
Oh my dear Tab.

*Lisa Wyatt (9)*
*Launceston CP School*

## MY CATS

My cats are crazy cats,
Curious and wild.
They dash and dive around my house,
Until they drive me wild.
My cats are ferocious cats,
Crazy and wild.
They chase their tails,
Round and round until they drive me wild.
And when I'm watching TV,
They curl upon my lap,
And then I say,
That is the end of those crazy
Cats until the next day.

*Chauntelle Besley (10)*
*Launceston CP School*


## WATER FROG

He springs with his feet
From lily to lily,
Straight across the lake.
Higher and higher in the air
And does not touch the water.
He croaks in a deep voice
To his friends
To get their attention.
Then they all come over and
Start to jump around.

*Adam Parnall (9)*
*Launceston CP School*

## A TIGER

Roaming through the jungle as king of beasts.
Slowly stalking around until he pounces on his prey.
His black and orange body gleams in the sun.
His stripes as black as night.
His eyes sparkle at dark.

*Kevin Hatch  (9)*
*Launceston CP School*


## THE WINDY DAY

Wind hammering against the window,
Trees falling over in the wind.
People getting cold,
Clouds speeding along.
Telephone wires getting damaged,
Electric gets cut off,
Candles give the only light.

*Thomas Arrowsmith  (9)*
*Launceston CP School*


## THE HAMSTER

It wakes from its little bed of straw,
It walks to the food, nibble, nibble,
Scampers round in the wheel,
Gets faster then slows down,
Scuttles to the bed,
The black and white hamster dozes.

*Joseph Pooley  (10)*
*Launceston CP School*

## ELECTRIC EEL

Prongs of light hitting the earth,
Fingers of white magic
Flashing in the angry night,
Drum rolls echoing fiercely.

Fear approaching,
The orchestra explodes,
As the eye of the storm closes in,
The flashes and drums unite.

The eye is ferocious,
Forking down its prey,
A blade of lightning,
A spitting blow blasting.

Running for shelter,
From the giant forky hand,
Firing light,
At the bewildered and homeless.

*Tom Potts  (10)*
*Launceston CP School*


## MY LITTLE BUDGERIGARS

My little budgerigars,
Soft and warm,
Beaks so yellow,
Fluffy like teddy bears,
Curl up to tennis balls in the night,
Sleep like a baby,
Bite like pins in your fingers.

*Emma Woodridge  (10)*
*Launceston CP School*

# RAP GRANDAD

I've got a grandad,
So big and bold,
He's the king of the sea,
So everyone's told.
He likes to go fishing,
Nearly every single day,
But the fish are always gone,
Because he's on his way.
I've got a grandad,
So big and bold,
He's the king of the sea,
So everyone's told.
When he gets to the docks,
He gets down upon the rocks,
He throws his line down deep,
Now he's got some fish to eat.
I've got a grandad,
So big and bold,
He's the king of the sea,
And I'm glad he's with me.

*Leanne Williams (10)*
*Launceston CP School*


# WINTER

White snow,
Ice, freezing ponds,
Wind humming against trees,
Snowflakes cantering to the ground,
Sharp draught.

*Michael Diebner (10)*
*Launceston CP School*

## BLACK MAMBA

Striking quickly,
The waiting lightning
Flashes brightly,
Diving again,
The rapid lights
Flare up the night sky.

Recharging for the next dart,
The deadly killer
Plummets towards the earth,
Finding its target,
The darting predator
Hits its bull's eye.

Enjoying its sport,
The jagged arrow
Loses its tension,
Flying through the air,
An unlucky victim
Fills the night air with his squeal.

*Matthew Parnall  (11)*
*Launceston CP School*


## RAMBO

My hamster Rambo,
Climbing on the bars like a tightrope walker,
And best of all . . .
To see him running in his ball,
Going so fast then, *bang! Smash!*
Into the wall.

*Timothy Strong  (9)*
*Launceston CP School*

## WRESTLING RAP

It's bad, it's cool,
It's wicked too.
Kane is the king of the wrestlers,
He stuns them all, he beats them up.
Crash, bang, wallop,
He throws them out,
He knocks them down,
He hates the rules,
He dislikes the boss and is always cross,
Crash, bang, wallop,
He never smiles, he never laughs,
And he always walks away,
Never talks to people,
He killed his brother,
Crash, bang, wallop.

*Karl Woodridge (11)*
*Launceston CP School*

## ALL ABOUT MY CAT

My cat is cuddly,
My cat is quiet,
He prowls all day, sleeps all night.
My cat is jet black and he has green eyes,
And he is always chasing butterflies.
My cat purrs when he is happy,
And he lies on my bed when he is sleepy.
I like my cat.

*David Striplin (10)*
*Launceston CP School*

## RAP WITH HELEN

Mrs Hudson she's so cool,
She's bad, she's wicked, she is no fool,
She loves to listen to music,
She always likes to choose it,
She never seems to give a flip,
'Cos she thinks she's always hip.

She's really radical,
She's really magical,
She's nutty, funky,
She's really punky,
At the end of the day,
We all say,
She is so cool,
She's nobody's fool.

*Lucy Addicott (10)*
*Launceston CP School*


## WOLF

As fast as the wind it zooms through the trees
Destroying anything in its way.
Swiftly swaying, feeling the breeze,
Unseen as it hunts its prey.
Fierce but silent as it crawls through the leaves,
Moving, crouching, hunting as it gets thinner.
When snow falls it starts to freeze,
Violently thinking its a winner.

*Kenny Channing (10)*
*Launceston CP School*

## KINGFISHER

Skilful and swift,
Graceful yet powerful,
With amazing agility,
Reaching for the sky.

A shrill cry,
Watching for a sign,
Ready to wake,
A compressed spring.

Speeding in all directions,
Darting and soaring,
Hovering then dropping,
A diving arrow.

*Thomas Brown (11)*
*Launceston CP School*




## SPARKY

Fast, alert and fierce,
She does not bite,
Likes a cuddle, and is good at tag.
Enjoys her food, and hates the cold,
Appreciates her photo being taken,
A good friend is opposite, Thumper the rabbit.
The colour of her fur is a chocolate brown,
She is a guinea-pig,
And her name is . . .
*Sparky.*

*Joshua Hall (10)*
*Launceston CP School*

# THE WIND'S COMPARISON

Soaring swiftly through the streets,
Picking its unsuspecting prey,
Carrying it through the transparent air,
Spying on the houses that line its path.

Whistling, howling, circling buildings,
Unstealthily as it flies through cities,
With strength enough to tip a car,
Spreading a deathly cold everywhere it goes.

Slyly creeping from town to city,
Over the country it soars,
Getting stronger as it flies,
Its talon-like grasp picking at the loose earth.

Scattering flocks of birds all over,
Soaring high above the ground,
Leaves like little animals, scattering everywhere,
Cutting through the clouds like a knife.

Dying down then coming back,
Getting stronger as it returns,
Developing from a small breeze to a sapling's nightmare,
When content it retreats only to terrify again.

*Thomas Adams (10)*
*Launceston CP School*

## KINGFISHER

Hovering in the fog of the sky,
Charging up,
Preparing for the descent,
Alert and ready to strike.

Then *flash!*
A squealing arrow
Descending towards the awaiting depths,
Prepared for battle.

It pierces the ripples,
Sending fear towards the helpless creatures,
Annihilating its victim,
It leaves the world behind.

***Edward Horn (11)***
***Launceston CP School***


## BLACK MAMBA

Swiftly striking its target,
Dancing to the sound of the thunder,
Carefully striking with all its might,
Slithering through the night,
Flashing before you,
Dodging everything in its path,
Waiting for its prey to come closer,
Flashing past like a quick typhoon,
Booming through the night flashing before your eyes.

***Nathan Jones (10)***
***Launceston CP School***

## THE DOLPHIN CALL

The dolphin moves softly and beautifully,
Her body moves in and out,
She plays cheerfully and makes a squeaking noise,
Catching fish to feed her baby.
My friend the dolphin makes no splash,
She uses her fins to propel her back home.
The calls of her baby make her swim
Towards her young one in their home.
But the baby is in trouble!
Mother makes a dash towards their home
To save her infant from an evil enemy.
She is too late,
The baby is gone,
The enemy is gone,
Forever.

*Georgina Freestone (9)*
*Launceston CP School*


## JAGUAR

Speeding through the trees,
Weaving amongst the grass,
Running fast and sleek,
Twisting, turning between the bushes,
Strong and muscular as it escapes,
Fierce and playful as it swoops,
Powerful and mighty, rustling leaves.

*Wayne Richter (10)*
*Launceston CP School*

## THE WILD PONY

A girl was walking in a field one day,
The grass was soaked with dew.
She heard a little whinnying neigh,
She turned around,
A silver stallion was standing there.
He stared at her with his pony eyes,
She stares back at him.
He takes a few steps closer,
Bows down and neighs to her.

She gets on his back,
He jolts into a trot.
The wind blows through her hair.
All she can do is hold on to his silky mane, so fair.
He stops, she gets off,
He trots along home.

The next day he came back again,
The girl likes the pony,
She knows she can't keep him.
She tells the pony to go on home.

She sadly watches him leave,
Never to see him again,
But every day she remembers
That wild, silver stallion
That followed her home.

*Amy Gathercole  (9)*
*Launceston CP School*

## LOCUST

Dancing over many nations,
A Destruction Derby,
Plaguing all Exodus countries,
Advancing in storm clouds.

Most violent ambush
Is the swarming assault,
Wildly killing crops,
Conducting a savage demonstration of destruction.

Days into a continuous night,
Devastating performance,
Revealing a cold-blooded exhibition
As they throw their vicious parties.

Mission complete,
Successfully damaged land,
The formation leave happy
To invade elsewhere.

*Lorna White  (11)*
*Launceston CP School*


## MY BIKE

My bike is silver,
I like riding it.
When I zoom up the road it feels
Like I'm flying.
When I zoom down the road the wind
Brushes against my face.

*Steven Smith  (10)*
*Launceston CP School*

## MY GRANDAD

My grandad's cool and he's wicked too,
He loves rollerblading just like you,
He's king of jokes,
He'll make you smile,
He's fit enough to run a mile.

Ha, ha, ha, hee, hee, hee,
That's my grandad as
Plain as can be.

When he sits down he'll get up again,
He's thin, he's cool, he's as tall as Big Ben,
He does his crosswords over again,
When he writes his diary he sits in his den.

Ha, ha, ha, hee, hee, hee,
That's my grandad as
Plain as can be.

When we go to parties where there's lots of dips,
My grandad will be there really quick,
So that's the story of my radical grandad,
I hope you were listening or he'll be sad.

*Geraldine Harris  (10)*
*Launceston CP School*


## THERE WAS AN OLD MAN

There was an old man from Spain,
Who lived in a carbon drain,
His pants fell down,
And blew up the town,
And that was the end of poor Wayne.

*Cassie Rowe  (10)*
*Liskeard Junior School*

## AN ALLITERATION

One:    wild watcher was weeping when William whizzed by.
Two:    terrible turtles tumbling towards the twisted trees.
Three:  thieves throwing things through the thick thunder thought
        theoretically that they were thwarted.
Four:   friends fighting furiously with fire-fighters.
Five:   farmers fetching their flocks from the field.
Six:    sausages sitting silently sizzling in the smelly saucepan.
Seven:  silver snakes slithering slowly in the scorching sand.
Eight:  elephants eating enormous ants.
Nine:   nifty nymphs nightly nose noisily knocking gnomes.
Ten:    tents totally terrible together trading trousers tonight.

*Axie Lavers (8)*
*Liskeard Junior School*


## NONSENSE NAMES

One wobbly wolf wandering in the wood.
Two twins twisting tweezers in the twilight.
Three threatening thugs thinking things.
Four folk follow fierce footballers.
Five friends find fishes to finish.
Six silly sisters sing similar songs.
Seven serious sea-divers search the sea for seals.
Eight experts eating eggs.
Nine nosy nomads knitting nice nighties.
Ten ticklish teenagers teasing terrible teachers.

*Lucy Rigby (9)*
*Liskeard Junior School*

## OVER THE HILLS AND FAR AWAY

Over the hills and far away,
Night-time owls come out to play,
Silently swooping on furry prey,
Never, never hunt by day.

Over the hills and far away,
Tree-based owls are glaring today,
Some are black, some are white,
Swallow food whole, not a bite.

Over the hills and far away,
Night-time owls come out to play.

*Ben Williams  (10)*
*Liskeard Junior School*

## DAFFODIL

Small,
sweet,
curved and tall,
still,
straight,
best of all,
flower,
so still,
it's a
daffodil.

*Heather Butt  (11)*
*Liskeard Junior School*

## THE BEACH

The beach is fun,
It's where children play.

They play in the sun,
They play all day.

The beach is fun,
It's where children play.

From waves they run,
Dodging the spray.

The beach is fun,
It's where children play.

They like to catch a tiny fish,
Not big enough to eat with chips on a dish.

The beach is fun.

*Lucy Williams  (10)*
*Liskeard Junior School*


## SUPER SIMPSON

I am Super Simpson,
I'm very, very strong.
I like to carry elephants,
I do it all day long.
I pick up about a dozen,
And hold them in the air.
It's really very simple,
For I have the strength to spare.

*Jamie Julian  (9)*
*Liskeard Junior School*

## SIMILES

As slow as a snail
I wrote.
As fresh as a daisy
I wrote.
As slippery as an eel
I wrote.
As cunning as a fox
I wrote.
As busy as a bee
I wrote.
As good as *me*
I wrote
Yes I did,
I wrote as good as Daniel,
But my teacher wouldn't believe me!

***Daniel Broster (10)***
***Liskeard Junior School***


## THE RACE

On the starting line, freshening up,
Getting ready for the cup.
A confident start by Linford Christie,
And Donovan Bailey in the fast lane three.

Coming up to the finishing line,
All six runners having a painful time.
Going for the best, first place,
Donovan Bailey wins the race.

***Guy Stroud (9)***
***Liskeard Junior School***

## WOMBLES

The Wombles have come,
Hip, hip, hooray!
The Wombles have come to clean up today!
Make way for the Wombles,
So they can Womble free.
Make way for the Wombles to clean our city!

The Wombles are furry,
The Wombles are brown.
The Wombles look up,
The Wombles look down.
The Wombles make good use of the things that they've found.
And Wombles clear litter all around!

Maybe the Wombles left Wimbledon Green
Because now there's nothing there to be cleaned!
With their small but powerful black nose,
The Wombles sniff out our rubbish by loads!
Now the Wombles are finished, they're off to Wimbledon Green,
The Wombles are finished and our city is clean.

I wonder why Wombles are so green?
Maybe it's just because they like being clean!

*Peter Little  (10)*
*Liskeard Junior School*


## WEATHER

It's pouring down with rain,
I wish I could go out,
I wish it would stop raining,
And the sun would come about.

The sun is shining high above,
Across the blue summer sky,
White fleecy clouds,
Are drifting by.

*Tamsin Job  (10)*
*Liskeard Junior School*


## A FIGHT

Joseph is my best friend,
He always works with me,
Our friendship will never end,
Until he copies me.
The teacher always tells me off,
It's not fair on me.
The teacher always tells me off,
It's not fair on me.
Joseph he does no wrong,
*She* always blames me.
Joseph always sits by me,
He likes to pick my brain.
But teacher thinks I copy him,
It's giving me real pain.
I waited for him at playtime,
I waited for my friend.
And I hit him really hard,
I hit him round the bend.
I was in at playtime, Joseph is not my friend,
It was not really my fault,
Joseph is *not* my friend.

*Adrian Vine  (9)*
*Liskeard Junior School*

# FERRARI

Zooming down the town,
a red flash in the sunlight,
disappearing fast.

Stopping at red lights,
going through the town traffic,
making people cry.

Very nice and loud,
breaking very, very fast
at the big Speed show.

The Speed show is big,
people get dust in their eyes,
people don't like it.

At last it is still,
it is a relief for them,
people say it's cool.

The driver steps out
and takes off his helmet,
and is it Damon Hill?

Did he win first prize?
He might have won, let's take a look,
yes, he really did.

People like driving,
it is really fun and cool,
so give it a try.

People liked that race,
I think they'll try it some time,
and find it is fun.

As a team you drive,
try and win the big medal,
people love it all.

*James Rowley (9)*
*Liskeard Junior School*


# Fox

Handsome man with a golden tail
Hunter without horse or hound
The feared, the fearful, the hunter, the hunted
Teeth sharp as a flint, a glint of his eye, a wisp of his tail and he's gone
The jumper, the runner, the digger.
Won't grin when hunting, won't sigh when merry
The sly trapper and poacher
The loving, caring father
A velvet black foot, an emerald green eye
A smart white chest, a razor of a claw.
A rustle in the bushes and he sees his prey
A young rabbit foolish enough to come his way
The pounce, the kill, the last cry of a young rabbit.
Spotted running hound at his heels
Beads of sweat falling, mingling with dew
Run round, not home but to the forest
Leaf green eyes red with anger
Down river on a floating log
Wave goodbye to hunt and dog
Down river, jump off, back home, safe.

*Jenny O'Connell (10)*
*Liskeard Junior School*

## FOOTBALL MISERY

Cooler than cool,
Is the game football.
Lack of control,
At the back of the ball,
Can cost a goal.
Kicking the ball all over the place,
With tremendous pace.
Running from end to end,
Through wind and rain.
What an exciting game.
The crowd cheer and stamp their feet,
I think they'd like a goal.
Oh that shot was very neat.
Time is nearly up,
One more try,
The ball flies in and hits the post.
The whistle blows,
We all walk off angrily,
Oh dear, I think we lost.

*Jonathan Cribb (10)*
*Liskeard Junior School*


## RAIN

Rain,
Rattling at windows,
Dripping on cars,
Smashing on the ground.
Rain!
Rain!
Coming from the clouds,
Rain! Rain! Rain!

*Daryl Hick (10)*
*Liskeard Junior School*

## THE FOX FAMILY

The fox is sleek,
With a bushy tail,
He's always sly,
As quick as a fly.

The fox's den,
(Sometimes called an earth),
Is the place where they give birth
To the little cubs.

I can hear them now,
The cubs' little bark
Drifting through the dark,
Like a howling wind.

But now the fox cubs
Are growing older,
They're growing big and bolder,
And it's time to move out.

One by one,
They leave the earth
To give birth
To their own family.

*Emma Hopkin  (10)*
*Liskeard Junior School*


## SPACE HAIKU

Comet in the sky,
Zooms across the galaxy,
Long tail disappears.

*Justin Hammond  (10)*
*Liskeard Junior School*

## HORSES

Horses are your friends
They like to eat grass from your hands,
Licking and crunching until it's all gone,
Then they want some more.

Horses gallop,
Horses trot,
Horses canter faster and faster.

Galloping horses racing from field to field,
Into the dark night racing horses,
Start to walk on their four feet
Listening to the howling wolves outside.

Horses are your friends.

*Anneka Johnson  (10)*
*Liskeard Junior School*


## DOLPHINS

Dolphins are blue and grey except
for the hourglass dolphin which is
black and white like the killer whale.

Dolphins have teeth as tiny as the end
of a pin, just right to eat fish. Dolphins
are the most intelligent mammals in the sea.

If we don't start using our brain
we will have to go to an
aquarium or a dolphin sanctuary.

*Leanne Delmonico  (10)*
*Liskeard Junior School*

## TORNADO

Thrashing through the fields so fast.
Breaking up the weather forecast.
Smashing everything in sight.
Mum's just had a very big fright.
Swirling, twirling, round and round,
Expanding as it comes from the ground.
Everything is settled now
I don't know how,
But it has gone.

*Patrick Devaney (9)*
*Liskeard Junior School*

## LION

I see a lion really sad,
God, it makes me really mad,
I see the hunters on the plain,
shooting at its lovely mane,
I see it lying on the floor,
dying, dying even more,
I see the family crowding around,
bowing their heads to the ground,
please God help me even more,
I see the lions on the floor.

*John Elkington (10)*
*Liskeard Junior School*

## GERBILS

Black and grey, cuddly,
Small and fluffy on your hands,
I love my gerbils.

My cat might get them,
The cat might eat them today,
I hope they don't die.

They will play with me,
Soot and Smoke are their names,
They love me a lot.

I feed them nice food,
Green, grey, pink, red and blue,
They eat it all up.

I love my gerbils.

*Jonathan Prinn  (9)*
*Liskeard Junior School*


## FRIENDSHIP

My best friend is the best ever,
We go nearly everywhere together.
Friendship.
We sometimes fall out,
But we don't really know what it's about.
Friendship.
We wear nearly everything the same,
And sometimes we have each other to blame,
When we're kept to last,
For mucking about in class.

*Hannah Mitchell  (9)*
*Liskeard Junior School*

## ERIC TAYLOR THE WAILER

Have you ever heard of Eric Taylor?
He was such a big wailer.
He wailed in the morning,
When the sun was coming out.
He wailed at lunch time,
While he was stuffing food in his mouth.
He wailed at night,
When the moon was shining bright.
But now he can't drink from a cup,
Because he drinks from a bottle.

Now Eric Taylor is grown up,
But he still can't drink from a cup.
And now he's got friends
Who also wail with him.
Eric Taylor is getting old and thinks
That wailing will solve his problems.
He lives on the streets now,
But everyone asks him how.
He manages to wail all through the day,
But he never answers their questions.

Now Eric Taylor is very old,
And the street that he lives on is very cold.
He still lives on the streets,
And has really, really long hair.
His parents have died,
His mother of a very strange asthma attack,
And his father of a heart attack.
Eric Taylor has a strain in his back,
There is sorrow with his friends,
As Eric Taylor suddenly dies.

*Sarah Kempster (9)*
*Liskeard Junior School*

## A POTION OF STRANGE, FUNNY RHYMES

These rhymes are so with the times,
I'm going to tell you them in verses,
Rip them from the book to make them fit in your purses.

Cat rhymes with bat,
Along with sat and hat,
Another two are floating into my mind.

A baboon went to the moon,
He saw a man who looked more like a prune,
Another two are whooshing by me on a rocket.

My mother took me to a museum,
It looked more like a painting I saw in New Zealand,
Two more are passing to and fro by satellite.

My last rhyme before I go, I created as easy as pie,
They're now flying low across the sky,
The last two are drifting by steadily and sadly.

Here I go with my rhyme,
I think I'll nibble on a bit of thyme,
All my rhymes have gone to pot, so I guess I'll just have to go.

*Stephanie Cayzer (9)*
*Liskeard Junior School*


## JAMIE C

I've got a best friend called Jamie C,
And he's got a girlfriend called Amy,
And they always go out to play,
Every, every, every day.

*Matthew Borlase (10)*
*Liskeard Junior School*

## RECIPE FOR THE ALL-TIME GREATEST FOOTBALLER

Part 1 - The Making
Take one right foot of Gianfranco Zola,
add with Shearer's left which will score every goal!
Mix with the stomach of Ronaldo very big and strong.
Drop in Roy Keane's mind and you won't go wrong.
Stir in Schmeichel's hands as big as tanks,
melt in Beckham's aim and you'll be at the bank!
And vitally Neville's arms as big as aircraft carriers,
and your player will be like a brick wall barrier.

Part 2 - The Game
I put my England kit on and walked out on the pitch,
I got ready to take kick-off but I had a stitch,
I passed the ball to Shearer, he passed back to Scholes,
Then came the hard bit, he set me up on goal!
I shimmied to the left and I shimmied to the right,
I took a swerving shot and scored with delight!
My England debut was simply ace,
But now I've got to wash my face!

*Tim Pearce (10)*
*Liskeard Junior School*


## PALM TREES

Bark as brown as varnished wood,
Palm leaves as green as grass,
Swaying in the gentle breeze,
Cooling the warm air,
Toasting their roots in the hot sand,
While gazing longingly at the transparent sea.

*Samantha Green (9)*
*Liskeard Junior School*

## THE OZONE LAYER

No one knows how long space is,
There may be a planet called St Liz
Planet Liz may have a mayor,
Well I don't know but forget the mayor,
We should look after our ozone layer.

Spray and gas both near and far,
And exhaust fumes from our car,
It all rises up in the air, but;
We should look after our ozone layer.

When we look on the news,
The ozone layer brings bad news,
The sun shines very hot,
People are suffering from the lot!
That's why we should look after our ozone layer.

*Paul Gale  (11)*
*Liskeard Junior School*

## SOMETIMES

Sometimes I am a real pig,
Sometimes I act very big,
Sometimes I am very rude,
Sometimes I am very good,
Sometimes I know I'm kind,
Sometimes I am kept behind,
Sometimes I wonder what I'll be,
Sometimes . . .

*Matthew Lindsay  (9)*
*Liskeard Junior School*

## DARKNESS

Darkness is creeping all around me
It's walking up the stairs.
Help! Help!
It's coming to get me
I hide under the covers.
Help! Help!
It's the darkness
Oh no!
It's put me in a sack
But soon I jump out
And run right back.
But now it's chasing me,
I don't know what to do
My face has gone black and blue.

*Kimberley Symons (7)*
*Liskeard Junior School*

## STARS

Stars,
Glittering white,
All through the night.
Up so high,
In the sky,
Pity there's no time to sit and stare.
Don't worry,
The stars will always be there!

*Kensa Vincent Garland (9)*
*Liskeard Junior School*

## POEMS

Why are poems so hard to write?
I wish I could go and fly my kite.
What should I write about? What should I do?
I know, I'll just ask to go to the loo.

'I'll do it for homework,' I said out loud,
Looking at a fluffy white cloud.
I'll do it after I watch TV,
After all I can't miss CBBC.

After tea I still didn't do it,
My dad said I had to keep fit.
So I took the dog out with me, out to the park,
Just for a bit of a walk and a bark.

When I got home, it was time for bed,
So I couldn't think of a poem off the top of my head.
That night I thought of lots of lines for my poem,
By breakfast, unfortunately, I'd forgotten them.

When I went to school that day,
I heard my teacher say,
'Oi! You, pay attention,
You have a lunch-time *detention!*'

*Naomi Parker  (10)*
*Liskeard Junior School*


## THE PISTOL

There was a young man from Bristol
Who always carried a pistol
He got his mail
Then was sent to jail
For his pistol fell out of his pocket.

When he got out of jail
He went home to open his mail
In one letter it said
Would you like a new bed
Because your old one got burned to the ground.

*Richard Cullingford  (11)*
*Liskeard Junior School*


## Fox

They are reddish-brown in colour,
They have a bushy tail.
Have you guessed yet?
    I am waiting.

They live in the woods.
Their lifespan is 12 years.
Have you guessed yet?
    I am waiting.

They live in holes,
Two metres underground.
Have you guessed yet?
    I am waiting.

They come out at night,
To give you a fright.
Have you guessed yet?
    I am waiting.

They like chasing rabbits,
To eat for their tea.
Have you guessed yet?
    No?
It's a *fox.*

*Nicola Oakes  (10)*
*Liskeard Junior School*

## FOOTBALL

When I grow up
I would like to be a goalie
For Manchester United.

I would be cheered
For a brilliant save.
I want to be saving
for United for years on.

When I grow up
I would like to be
A midfield player
For England.
The crowd would jump up
From their seats
When I score a goal.

*Tom Peters  (11)*
*Liskeard Junior School*

## A LIMERICK

There was an old woman from Spain,
Who lived in a house down a lane,
She slept with her cat,
Always wore her hat,
And her little dog was a pain!

*Katy Stone  (10)*
*Liskeard Junior School*

## OLD TRAFFORD

The fans enter the stadium
The lights shine on the pitch
Players get ready for kick-off
And minutes after goals go flying by
Then players get badly injured.

*Mathew Jenkins (11)*
*Liskeard Junior School*


## SHOGUN WARRIOR CHIEF

Ninja-kick, sword-stab,
Shogun-warrior, fighting fab,
Japanese land he protects,
Killing off enemies, he detects.
Alert! Alert! Enemy attack!
Sneak upon them from around the back.
Use your special fighting skills,
Stab them in the back, I'll tell you it kills!

*Robert Peters (10)*
*Liskeard Junior School*


## PLANE

Planes in the sky having a race
Plane like a bird in the sky
Plane in the sky going here and there
Planes in the sky having a race
Plane in the air flying everywhere.

*Andrew Wilkinson (11)*
*Liskeard Junior School*

## IN THE DARK

Dark, dark, dark
I'm not frightened,
You can eat me,
But if you do,
You will be sorry.

*Shawny George (7)*
*Liskeard Junior School*

## DARKNESS

In a dark, dark town,
there is something,
creeping around.
I was frightened
I ran,
I was too fast,
I was eaten,
I was never seen again.

*John Burns (7)*
*Liskeard Junior School*

## HAMSTER

A hamster running in its running wheel,
Has to stop to make a meal.
Nuts and seeds and bits of weeds,
A healthy diet that's what it needs.

A hamster likes to run and play,
But a hamster always runs away.
He comes along here and comes along there,
But make sure he doesn't get in your hair.

*James Mitchell (10)*
*Liskeard Junior School*


## DARKNESS

Darkness is scary,
It will leap up on you,
It scares me,
It frightens me,
It frightens my pets,
It will not leave us alone,
My brother hates the dark,
He needs a light in his bedroom
Or it will smother him.

*James Cobb (8)*
*Liskeard Junior School*


## DARK

Dark, dark, dark,
I'm scared of the dark
Help, help,
It is eating me.
I am dead
My spirit has left my body
Eeeek
My body is on the floor
A man sees me dead.

*Natasha Pearce (8)*
*Liskeard Junior School*

## MANCHESTER UNITED SQUAD

Schmeichel is a mighty Dane,
Berg works hard again and again,
Neville throws like nothing's there,
Irwin runs like a tornado, yeah,
Pallister is as tall as St Paul's,
Keane's aggressive 'cos he makes the rules,
Beckham's shot curls like bent lead,
Butt can run and use his head,
Giggsy's speed is quite frightening,
And Sheringham's feet, more than skill,
And Cole changes the score when it's nil-nil.

*Nicky Joys  (10)*
*Liskeard Junior School*




## GHOSTS

Ghosts are lurking in my house
but I can only hear a mouse.
My house is haunted and that is true
well it's true for me and you.
A familiar smell blew up my nose
it's the smell of death that rose.
Help me out I'm stuck inside
please don't leave me to decide.

*Adam Kingston  (10)*
*Liskeard Junior School*

## DOLPHIN

The dolphin jumps,
His tail flickers,
He has charm
As the graceful animal leaps
Through the air,
A silky and shiny skin
Sleek movement
When the dolphin
Jumps through the sky.

*Freya Lemon  (10)*
*Liskeard Junior School*


## VICTORIAN FACTORY GIRL

As I work in the factory
As I work in the factory
Me back is aching some
Me back is aching some
The slashes on me back
The slashes on me back
I hate it here
I hate it here
I do.

*Marcus Jeffery  (11)*
*Liskeard Junior School*

## DARKNESS

Black is blue,
Blue is black,
Turn around,
It's coming for you.

*Kye Griffin  (7)*
*Liskeard Junior School*


## DARKNESS

In a dark dark house
It is black and scary
I smell something weird
There is something behind me
I smell something scary
It smells like soap.

*Arthur Smith  (7)*
*Liskeard Junior School*


## DARKNESS BLACK

At night it's darkness all around
Bats flying to the ground.
I have a fright
When I turn on the light
I'm very scared in the night
It gives me a fright.
It scares me to see it standing there
It scares me downstairs,
It follows me out the back.

*Zara Edmondson  (8)*
*Liskeard Junior School*

## DARKNESS

Soot falls down the chimney
As the wind howls.
The black cat stands at the window
Making funny noises.
The fox searches in dustbins
As the bat flies around.
Darkness makes me shiver
Darkness leads on to a wonderland.
What am I feeling
It could be a spider,
It could be a tarantula!

*Matthew Foster  (8)*
*Liskeard Junior School*


## DARKNESS

It's dark I'm all alone,
There's a cat on my ceiling,
I hope it's not real!
Shall I get out of bed,
Will Mum hear me creeping?
Get on the top bunk,
Go on the top bunk,
I touch my ceiling
It is not real,
It is morning
It is nothing to be afraid of.

*Melanie Bowden  (8)*
*Liskeard Junior School*

## DARKNESS

What do I see?
What do I hear?
I only see dark all around me,
Creeping all around the room.
It hides things,
Oh no
It is going in my wardrobe
To go back to sleep.

*Heather-Rose Pedler  (7)*
*Liskeard Junior School*

## DARKNESS

Blue, black,
I'm coming for you,
Turn around,
I will swallow you.

*Craig Dawe  (7)*
*Liskeard Junior School*

## DARKNESS

Dark, dark, black around me,
Creeping all over me.
It scares me,
It frightens me,
There's a spider crawling around my room.

*Jessica Parnell  (8)*
*Liskeard Junior School*

## DARKNESS

Dark is black, dark is blue
It'll eat you in a stew
Are you afraid of the dark?
I am
I bet you
Rats and bats and howling cats
Come out at night
King snakes come too
They eat the sweet mice.

*Adam Whittington (8)*
*Liskeard Junior School*


## SILLY TALES

One wild wig warned William
Two twisted toads told tales
Three thin thrushes threw thistles
Four fat firemen flapping at flames
Five flat flies falling
Six sizzling school sausages sat in a saucepan
Seven screeching seagulls see a seal
Eight astonished ants act an adventure
Nine new nails are never noisy
Ten terrible tents tear with terror.

*Peter Cole (9)*
*Liskeard Junior School*

## AN ALLITERATION

One walrus walking warmly wondering wistfully
Two Tudors thieving trowels
Three terrific terrapins tricking turtles
Four fantastic foxes fidgeting with ferocity
Five fish fascinating frogs
Six shellfish shaking after a shipwreck
Seven sharks spying on Sam
Eight enormous eagles are their prey
Nine naughty newts nibble
Ten toddlers being tickled by a teddy.

*Ian Hicks  (9)*
*Liskeard Junior School*




## TWIRLING TALES

One worried walrus wondered what was what
Two terrifying turtles threatened thick thieves
Three thinking thugs think through their thin thing
Four ferocious ferrets fought friendly figures
Five fuming fathers fought Fred Thumb
Six sinking ships sunk to the sea
Seven singing singers sang a song
Eight eating elephants nibbling enormous Easter eggs
Nine naughty newts nibbling nuts
Ten tinging tins tanging mad.

*Adam Nance  (9)*
*Liskeard Junior School*

## DARKNESS

Darkness is around me,
Help I'm scared
I hear something,
It's behind me,
It's in my cupboard,
It's barking around me
And snuggling around me.

*Tristan Greaney (7)*
*Liskeard Junior School*


## ELECTRICITY

Electricity is like
the sun which is dangerous.
Electricity is like a spider's web
as it runs from a power station.
Electricity is vicious.
It can be kind by bringing life.

*Jasmine Gregory (8)*
*Liskeard Junior School*


## AN ELECTRIC POEM

Electric is like a tiger
A leaping vicious tiger
Zap buzz it goes
Volts and battery run away
The tiger is a friendly creation.

*Lucy Banyard (8)*
*Liskeard Junior School*

# ELECTRICITY

Electricity is like a tiger
Roaring through the cables.
It is vicious too
But it can also be a friendly thing
That gives a buzzing sound.
As it passes by
It gives us life
It gives us light.

*Keighlee Bell (8)*
*Liskeard Junior School*


# ELECTRICITY

Electricity is like a very little person going around the world
He clicks his fingers and makes electricity work
Electricity kills but also gives us a life
Be careful with electricity
It will hurt you
Don't put loads of plugs on the same socket
Make sure you don't put your drink on electricity.

*Kayleigh Stacey (9)*
*Liskeard Junior School*


# ELECTRICITY

Electricity is like a helping hand
It can help you do things like
Cook your food
It can keep your house warm
But it can kill.

*Nathan Binder (9)*
*Liskeard Junior School*

## ELECTRICITY

Electricity is like a tiger
If you have a light
Sometimes it's dull
Or powerful
Powerful is when
It glows quite well
And dull when
It does not
Work quite well
It's dangerous when
You touch electricity
It will kill.

*Gemma Williams  (9)*
*Liskeard Junior School*

## THE ELECTRIC LION

Electricity is like a lion
It hunts and it kills
It comes near you ready to pounce and eat
Electricity is dangerous
I hope it won't get me
It can run fast and creep slow
It dies when wet
That's when it is dangerous
Electricity is dangerous
I hope it won't get me.

*James Griffiths  (8)*
*Liskeard Junior School*

## ELECTRICITY

Electricity is like your best friend
when you treat it the right way.
Electricity can kill you
by putting too much power in the socket.
Electricity is like a helping hand
it helps us when we need it.
Electricity is like a wild animal
hunting in your house.
Electricity is like veins
it flows through the house.
Electricity and water just don't mix.
*Be careful.*

*Karla Spargo  (9)*
*Liskeard Junior School*


## ELECTRICITY

Electricity is like blood,
Because it flows and gives life,
Electricity can give and take life,
It can be friendly, it can be rough,
Electricity is powerful,
It can also be dull.
Electricity is stored in a battery,
It can give you a very bad zap.
Electricity can be your friend
If you treat it the right way.

*Adam Clargo  (9)*
*Liskeard Junior School*

## ELECTRICITY POEM

Electricity is like,
A leopard.
It goes buzzing,
Through the wires,
Really really quick.
Electricity is very active,
It gives us life,
Like the sun,
It makes important things
Work.
It goes in circulation,
All around the country.

*Adrian Sleeman (9)*
*Liskeard Junior School*

## ELECTRICITY

Electricity is like veins,
It gives life and can kill,
Electricity flows through the world
And gives help,
Electricity buzzes through wires,
Electricity is like a gush of wind
Like a hurricane,
Electricity gives a computer life
To work.

*Donna Leng (9)*
*Liskeard Junior School*

## ELECTRICITY

Electricity is like a helping hand
Because it gives light.
It's active like a meander
It needs batteries
And wires
Zap! It sounds like a television
It's got a big circuit
Ouch! Somebody forgot
To put the resistor on
It gives information
It's a computer.

*Charlotte Coad (9)*
*Liskeard Junior School*


## ELECTRICITY

Electricity is like a tiger
Roaring through the wires.
Electricity is like a helping hand
Light, TV, computer and Hoover plug
Are all worked by electricity.
It gives life and can kill you
Electricity is dangerous.
It is like a web going through the wire
Through the streets into our homes.

*Claire Knight (9)*
*Liskeard Junior School*

## ELECTRICITY

Electricity is like a meander
It flows through the wires and makes life
It is vicious like a tiger
It kills all living things on earth
It is like a friendly helping hand
And gives life to all electrical things
For human beings on earth
It *zaps* them for a warning
And kills them as well
It is very powerful
So if you touch it you'll be stung
And you'll die.

*Michael Williams  (9)*
*Liskeard Junior School*

## ELECTRICITY

Electricity is like a lion,
It's vicious, it kills.
Electricity is a computer,
It's friendly, it's kind.
Electricity is like the sun,
It's powerful and hot.
Electricity's like a vein,
It holds life and death.

*Richard Hargraves  (9)*
*Liskeard Junior School*

## THE MATCH

Walking to the footie field all tense and ready to play,
Waiting in my footie kit.
I am about to play
I'm in my final position the whistle is about to go
Finally football takes place and our team scores a goal
I'm running into the penalty box and I am passed the ball
The number ten comes up to me and puts me on the floor
The ref calls a penalty for then I score a goal
The whistle goes two-nil to us
The other team goes without a fuss.

*Daniel Daw  (11)*
*Liskeard Junior School*


## SPACE

Space is dark,
      It's never ending
           It keeps on going,
                Never ending,
                    This way,
              That way,
           Never ending,
      Space is spooky,
Never ending,
      Spacecraft moving
           Through never ending space.

*Emma Banyard  (11)*
*Liskeard Junior School*

## HORSE

See how he jumps
Over high things
See how he runs
Through rivers and streams
See how he gallops
Through orchards and fields
See how he eats
As quick as a flash
See how he drinks
From the pond
See how he sleeps
So softly and still
See how he loves
His oats so golden
See how the stallion
Loves to be patted
See how his hooves
Go clip clop, clip clop
See how he shines
In sparkling sun.

*Sarah Knight (11)*
*Liskeard Junior School*


## FIRE NED

He has flames on his head
And two hundred yellowy sparks
He has charcoal for eyes
And a yellowy surprise
As he walks down the street at night.

*Joseph Michael Squire*
*Liskeard Junior School*

## I LOVE ANIMALS

I've got lots of animals
A hamster and some fish,
A dog that eats his food from a bowl
A cat that drinks from a dish.

I love animals
And I am very lucky,
Because I live on a farm with pigs
And when we feed them, we get mucky.

I care about animals
Very very much,
We've got a horse
With a very soft touch.

*Lisa Rendall  (11)*
*Liskeard Junior School*


## WALKING

Walking down the lane,
Legs pushing up and down,
Pounding the ground like pistons,
Knees quickly bending at their joints,
Every time the leg is lifted.
I wish I still had legs,
For now I am sitting in a wheelchair
For life!

*Dylan Devaney  (11)*
*Liskeard Junior School*

## MY HORSE

See how he gallops through rivers and
streams,
See how he trots through fields to his
dreams,
See how he jumps over walls and high
fences,
Past bins and trees and jumps over
benches,
See how he canters his hooves touch the
ground,
See how he trots and walks all
around.

*Natasha Humphries  (11)*
*Liskeard Junior School*

## SQUIRRELS

See how she leaps,
From tree to tree before she rests,
See how she climbs,
Through her dark forest,
Walking through the wood crunching on twigs,
See how she digs,
To bury her berries,
When people go past eating cherries,
See how she runs through the leaves,
Swinging her tail up into the trees.

*Rebecca Mole  (11)*
*Liskeard Junior School*

## You're The Top!

You're the top!
You're my best pet
Awake at night and sleep in the day
A cream colour
A fudge colour
A huge sunflower seed
You're the top!
In the wheel you tread all night
Waking me up
Banging his food bowl up and down
You're the top!
You're Fudge
You're my hamster.

*Kelly Cowling (11)*
*Liskeard Junior School*


## Fire

*Bonfire*
People gathering around small and big fires
People eating toffee apples
Fireworks setting off making big explosions.

*Burning trees*
People chopping trees
Making fire for their warmth
Burning marshmallows.

*Keeping warm*
People gathering around fires
Inside houses
Keeping warm whenever they want.

*Andrew Barnes (11)*
*Liskeard Junior School*

## DOLPHINS

Shiny backs glisten
From the sea,
Grey with little specks of white
Gliding through the water
With a smile in the night.

When they dive
Their bodies are curved and round
Playing, splashing out of bound.

Catching food
For them to eat
They can swim with humans
And it's pretty neat.

*Siobhan Howe  (11)*
*Liskeard Junior School*


## OUT IN THE COUNTRY

A glistening tail his wings outspread
And bends a narrow golden head,
Getting ready for the kill
The eagle keeps its body still.

Slipping and sliding as he goes
While all around a strong wind blows,
Slithering silent without a sound
The snake moves quickly along the ground.

A bushy tail his fur so red
In a ditch he makes his bed,
Trotting swiftly through the fields
The fox hops fences landing on its heels.

*Ashley Stroud  (11)*
*Liskeard Junior School*

## MY SPECIAL PLACE

My special place is my bedroom
I can lock the door
My sister and mum can't come in
I look out my window
Listen to the wind and birds
I watch the cars go by
I have my music on.

My special place is my nan's house
I put on the television,
But I don't watch it,
I look around the room thinking about things,
I like my nan's house; it is really cosy.
She always has the fire on,
Nan has very soft chairs
So I go to sleep on them
Always.

*Emma Litherland (9)*
*Liskeard Junior School*

## SPACE

Space is empty, no one living there
Rockets in the air flying everywhere
Space is empty, no one living there
No plants are growing there
Space is empty, no one living there
No oxygen in the air
Space is empty, no one living there.

*Nathan Barker (11)*
*Liskeard Junior School*

## POLAR BEARS

Polar bears roam the mountains,
Mountains as tall as Big Ben,
Feet as warm as carpet,
Pads the icy ground again.

Eyes as clear as crystal,
Teeth as sharp as knives,
Claws as sharp as nails,
In an icy cave he lies.

*Amy Rigby  (11)*
*Liskeard Junior School*

## ANGER

Anger is hot and frightening,
Anger is full of fear,
Anger is when I'm really cross
And smoke comes out my ear.
Anger is my brother kicking me,
It makes me go bright red,
He always teases me a lot,
And gets me sent to bed!

*Jessica Ryder  (9)*
*Lostwithiel JI School*

## POLLUTION

P ollution is litter dropped down onto the ground contaminating
   all around.
O zone layer breaking down, more harmful rays shining down.
L akes, rivers and oceans full of chemicals poisoning fish and animals -
   food chain going wrong.
L andfill sites overflowing - too much rubbish to bury in the ground.
U nderstand the dangers of rubbish on our earth.
T ime's getting short, we'd better do something soon.
I think that we all want a green and healthy planet to live on.
O ur mission is to take some action.
*N ow!*

*Zinzi Graham (8)*
*Lostwithiel JI School*


## ANGER

A is the red-hot letter that starts the fearsome word,
N is the second letter like an eagle bird,
G is the third letter like a spicy sauce,
E is the fourth letter like tiger's claws,
R is the last letter, flaming hot, red,
   Well that is my poem just as I said.

*Stephanie Newton (9)*
*Lostwithiel JI School*

## POLLUTION

P lease keep the world clean,
O il out of the sea,
L ooking after our world,
L ooks after me.
U se all the bins and,
T idy up the tins,
I f you start to think about it,
O r sit and wonder why,
N ow all the wildlife might have gone
    and we haven't said, 'Goodbye.'

*Patrick Barclay (9)*
*Lostwithiel JI School*

## POLLUTION

Polluted rivers with cans and rubbish,
Old rotten apples too.
Litter in the countryside.
Litter in the sea,
Up in the air the sky is no longer blue.
Through the brown and mucky water
Insects struggle to get out,
Oceans covered in tar and oil,
Never throw rubbish about.

*Sarah Wigley (8)*
*Lostwithiel JI School*

## POLLUTION

Pollution is caused by people,
Other animals get hurt,
Lots of animals get stuck in things,
Lots of animals get trapped under things.
Under the sea, lobsters get hurt,
Tortoises get cut by things,
I understand about not throwing litter,
Oh! Stop throwing litter,
Nobody drop litter, please!

*Talisa Powell  (9)*
*Lostwithiel JI School*

## POLLUTION

P  ollution is terrible, it spreads
     germs everywhere,
O  ught to be stopped, so there!
L  itter dropped on the ground
L  eaves a mess all around.
U  nless you start helping,
T  he earth might start dying.
I  n future don't be mean
O  r carry on being unclean,
N  ever pollute the earth!

*Jennifer Jezard  (9)*
*Lostwithiel JI School*

## LAST WEEK

On Monday I decided to go to the jungle.
On Tuesday I made a secret camp.
On Wednesday I met a cheerful jaguar.
On Thursday we played jaguar spots and stripes.
On Friday I made a boat out of winding, weeping willow trees.
On Saturday I slept in my beautiful boat all day with the jaguar
    as my pillow.
On Sunday we sailed home to mum and I hid the jaguar under my bed!

*Tabitha Rattray  (8)*
*Marazion CP School*

## SPIDERS!

I am the climber that bites.
I am the climber of the web.
I hide away waiting for my prey.
I am a monster to a fly.
I wrap them up like Christmas presents.
My web is my silver floor.
I am a dark, dark rainbow.
When I get hungry I unwrap my
juicy presents one by one.

*Hannah Willey  (8)*
*Marazion CP School*

## SPIDER

I am called Hunter.
I creep around looking for juice and bugs.
I climb up my web with my hairy legs one
$$\text{by}$$
$$\text{one}$$

I pounce so lightly not even the blood of my prey
can hear me.
I wait for my supper so still, so patient.
And when the fly comes to the web I am ready.
Then I crunch and I chew and my dinner is always delicious.

*Cathryn Wilcock  (9)*
*Marazion CP School*

## WHAT IS BLACK?

Black is death waiting for your wet blood.
Black is creeping from grave to grave.
Black is a tunnel for you to walk through.
Black is a whale that takes you for a ride into the deep.
Black is a witch's cauldron, a steamy hot potion.
Black is a motorbike's tyre spinning in the mud.
Black is a crow's feather floating from the sky.
Black is a hand on a clock that has just struck midnight.

*Luke Whitford  (9)*
*Marazion CP School*

## THE DAISY

Petals like snowflakes falling.
Or a swan swimming on a pond.
Or a feather falling from a dove.
An umbrella opening in the rain.
A nest of golden birds.

*Becky Stains  (8)*
*Marazion CP School*


## THE AUTUMN WIND

The autumn wind throws our hats away.
The autumn wind rattles the post-box like a baby with a toy.
The autumn wind digs the slates off the roof.
The autumn wind tap-dancing on the window and chasing
the waves out to sea.

*Matthew Andrews  (8)*
*Marazion CP School*


## WANTED - BABY BOY BAIGLE

Baby boy Baigle is as tall as fire.
Baby Boy Baigle has hair as black as ebony.
Baby Boy Baigle's eyes swirl like a Catherine wheel.
Baby Boy Baigle jumps like a kangaroo.
Baby boy Baigle laughs like a witch.
Baby Boy Baigle has a nose like a pin.
Baby Boy Baigle dances like the wind.
Baby Boy Baigle walks like a lady.

*Bryony Dodson  (9)*
*Marazion CP School*

## My Mum

*Who* makes me as lucky as a dime?
*Who* makes me warm as the breeze blowing in June?
*Who* makes me laugh like a monkey?
*Who* makes me feel as spoilt as a Christmas present?
*Who* makes me happier than a lottery winner?
*Who* makes me as special as a star?
*Who* makes me as happy as a dolphin?
            *Mum* does!

*Scott Barberry  (8)*
*Marazion CP School*


## One, Two, Three . . .

One wild, wonderful woman watched wise wizards.
Two tiny tadpoles, tiptoed to Taunton.
Three tigers terrified, ten thoughtful teachers.
Four farm factories, faded from floating fishermen.
Five fuzzy, frightful, flasks, fixed floppy footballs forever.

*Treve Beckerleg  (7)*
*Marazion CP School*


## The Daisy

A little white broom sweeping
the grass on a spring day.
An arm reaching up.
Or an ear listening to the sky.
The petals like hair to keep its
precious eye warm.

*Alfred Tiley  (8)*
*Marazion CP School*

## WANTED

Tiger the whiner has hair like a punk
and his teeth are as black as a storm.
Tiger the whiner laughs like a goat
and his bristles are a bed of nails.
Tiger the whiner is as tall as a skyscraper
with eyes as blue as the sea.
Tiger the whiner is as greedy as a pig
and his clothes are scruffy like a tramp.
Tiger the whiner walks like a pigeon
with a scar on his cheek like a torn ship sail.
Tiger the whiner has a nose like a witch.
*Have you seen this man?*

***Kieran Knight  (9)***
***Marazion CP School***


## THE DAISY IN JANUARY

A wine glass in gentle hands.
Feathers on a magic dove flying in the sky of grass.
A king's crown resting on a throne.
Golden eyes watching you.
Petals like teeth, chattering on a cold day.
A golden baby crawling in a white bed.
Or a broom of petals sweeping the morning open.

***Briony Sedgeman  (8)***
***Marazion CP School***

## A DARK, DARK NIGHT

On a dark, dark night,
When the stars were bright,
I went into my garden.
What did I see?
Two green eyes were looking at me,
What did I hear?
A swish of a tail,
And a crying wail,
She's run up a tree,
And is staring at me.
Call her down into the house.
Curved and floppy,
Warm and soppy,
Quiet as a mouse.

*Emma Milton  (9)*
*Mylor Bridge Primary School*

## A WINDY DAY

The wind it makes me shiver and quiver,
As the wind strikes my face,
The doors are banging,
The wind is whooshing,
As it gets stronger.

Trees are swaying,
Like fingers pointing the way.
I think it's going to be like this all day.
Daffodils dancing in the breeze,
I think I'm going to sneeze.

I'm finally inside, phew!
I'm sitting by the fire.
The wind is howling out there,
But I don't care.

*Debbie Thomas  (9)*
*Mylor Bridge Primary School*


## AT THE BOTTOM OF MY GARDEN

At the bottom of my garden,
In the middle of the night,
I can see something creeping,
In the gloomy light.
Long black fur and silent paws,
Twitching nose and whiskers,
And eyes as bright as stars.

At the bottom of my garden,
In the middle of the night,
It jumps upon the garden wall,
And gives a mouse a fright.
It scurries through the undergrowth,
Rustling through the fallen leaves,
And wonders where the mouse can be.

At the bottom of my garden,
In the middle of the night,
The clouds pass by the moon,
And the stars are twinkling bright.
An owl hoots, the animal scoots,
And in comes my black cat,
To sit beside the fire.

*Hannah Sly  (9)*
*Mylor Bridge Primary School*

## THE ZIZZER, ZAZZER AND THE ZACKEYON

Ton Ton beware the Zizzer Zazzer and the Zackeyon,
For they bring dangers in the foggly wood.
Ton Ton went through the foggly, bobby and loggy wood.
With his blazing deadly sharp sword,
He rested against the Ping Dong rock.
With eyes of flame and sinning horns,
Came the frightening Zizzer Zazzer
Glumpthing to the Tong Pong tree
Whilst Ton Ton was having his tea.
Ton Ton jumped up and drew his blazing sword,
1,2,1,2, and 3 and then snip, snap
The Zizzer Zazzer's head came off!
Ton Ton went on his way home,
When out jumped from the swessy wessy bersh,
With two heads darting and eyes of flowing lava,
Came the incredible Zackeyon,
Stretching its claws as sharp as pins,
Towards Ton Ton who was shaking dizzily.
Ton Ton once again drew his blazing sword
1,2,1,2, and 3 and then snip, snap,
The Zackeyon darted in and out.
With its big strong wings it dived at Ton Ton,
And killed him straight away.
Ton Ton you weren't aware of the Zackeyon,
And now you lie dead in the foggy wood.

*Philip Merrifield  (9)*
*Mylor Bridge Primary School*

## THE WIND

Invisible giant
Rocking the trees,
Making you feel
Like you will freeze.

Ripples gliding
Across the water,
Leaves blowing
Across the mortar.

Hounds howling
To get indoors,
Scratching with
Invisible paws.

*Freddie Brown  (8)*
*Mylor Bridge Primary School*

## I WORK IN EGYPT

I'm boiling and sweaty,
No time to stop.
I feel cross and angry,
As I do this job.
I struggle on the boat,
To fetch a load,
I wish I was home where I belong.
I'm horrible and sticky,
As I go down the River Nile.
I work in Egypt.
All day long,
From sunrise to sunset.

*Penny Dale  (8)*
*Mylor Bridge Primary School*

## NIGHT-TIME

Late last night,
I heard an owl hooting,
But I could see nothing,
In the gloomy night.
Slowly my eyes became accustomed,
To the dim light.
Gradually I could see,
Stars twinkling in the sky,
Monster looking trees,
Waving their arms,
In the light of the moon.
There's a rustling in the leaves,
A cat searching for mice,
I can hear a frog croaking,
While the river rushes on its way.
It's getting cold,
In the dim light of the moon.

*Erin Bastian  (9)*
*Mylor Bridge Primary School*


## TESSIE

A mad licker,
A good barker,
A fast runner,
A ball catcher,
A loud howler,
A deep sleeper,
A nice cuddler,
That's my dog
        Tessie.

*Paul Keeble  (8)*
*Mylor Bridge Primary School*

## DARK IN THE GRAVEYARD

Dark in the graveyard,
A new ghost haunts
Around and around all the graves,
Waking up all the other slaves.

Dark in the graveyard,
Frankenstein stamps
With a bolt in his neck
That goes clank, clank, clank.

*Dark in the graveyard*
*Don't go there*

For you might get a great big

*Scare!*

**Tom Phipps  (9)**
**Mylor Bridge Primary School**


## DARKNESS

Dark in the bedroom, it's dark and scary,
At midnight I am asleep
Whilst outside in the garden
Dark in the night, the badgers creep.
The stars twinkle, the moon shines,
Whilst deep in the wood
Dark in the night, the owls swoop,
The trees crinkle and crackle,
Whilst dark in my bedroom,
I am asleep.

**Ross Timmins  (8)**
**Mylor Bridge Primary School**

## THE WIND

The wind is howling,
There's a breeze on my face,
Blowing branches like witches' fingers,
Faces glowing,
                    What do I see?
I see daffodils dancing,
Trees rustling,
                    What do I hear?
I hear leaves tossing and turning,
Branches swaying,
                    How do I feel?
I feel cold, shivery,
Fingers all numb,
                    Where do I stroll?
I walk to the pool,
The ripples look like wrinkled cling film.

*Sarah Phillips  (9)*
*Mylor Bridge Primary School*


## THE PHARAOH'S TOMB

Sweltering, sweating all day long,
Scared, tired, hungry and thirsty.
Can't stop, can't talk,
Blocks are heavy, blocks are huge.
Pull, pull across the sand,
Heaving towards the pyramid.
The pyramid stands great and tall
Towering above us,
Making us feel small.
It's almost finished,
Ready for the Pharaoh's tomb.

*Tamara Tubb  (7)*
*Mylor Bridge Primary School*

## THE WIND

The wind is cold,
The trees are moving.
I am feeling freezing,
I can hear the wind howling.
The leaves are rustling
I can see daffodils dancing,
The birds are flying.
Branches are moving and swaying,
The water ripples when you pass,
I am feeling warmer,
Because I'm inside at last.

*Wayne Falcus  (9)*
*Mylor Bridge Primary School*


## A DRAGON

A fire breather,
A tail flicker,
With a scaly tummy.
A bush disguiser,
A leopard eater,
With a flaming tongue.
A house crasher,
A noise maker,
With a bright yellow eye.
It's a dragon coming out of the sky.

*Emma Roberts  (8)*
*Mylor Bridge Primary School*

## MY BROTHER

A great pesterer,
A lot of trouble,
Good at spelling,
A constant whiner,
And a brilliant game player.
A sister annoyer,
And a big bully,
An elephant upstairs,
As he stamps around when he's upset.
That's my brother!

*Jessica Bugden  (8)*
*Mylor Bridge Primary School*

## AT NIGHT

One windy night,
I got a big fright,
But it was only a fox,
Snuffling in a box.

One windy night,
I saw the trees swaying,
In the wind and the breeze,
They swung with ease.

Be careful at night,
You could get a big fright,
Because there's no light,
To help you with your eyesight.

*Jonathan Cook  (9)*
*Mylor Bridge Primary School*

## WIND

The wind is cold,
Like a freezer.
Leaves are blowing around me.
The swimming pool is scary,
In the howling wind.
The wind is blowing down the chimney,
Like a big animal.
The wind is roaring around me.
I'm going in,
And that's where I'm staying!

*Thomas Everton  (8)*
*Mylor Bridge Primary School*

## OUT OF MY WINDOW

Out of my window,
The cold wind blows,
Owls call haunting noises.

Out of my window,
The tractors growl,
And the early cockerel crows.

Out of my window,
The silver moon shines,
Over the moonlit fields.

*James Hill  (9)*
*Mylor Bridge Primary School*

## My Baby Brother

A naughty smacker,
A little screamer,
A night yeller,
A constant whinger,
A Teletubby watcher,
A doggy lover,
A good sneaker,
An angry fighter,
A silly swimmer,
A trouble maker,
An excellent terror,
A naughty puncher,
A bad skater,
It's got to be my baby brother.

*Rachael Vinnicombe (8)*
*Mylor Bridge Primary School*

## Don't Go Out At Night

Don't go out at night,
For you might have a fright.
Owls squeaking in the trees,
Rats running around,
Cars zooming down the road,
Bats flapping on the roof,
Cats howling in the bushes,
Dogs barking in the dark,
Lots of things to give you a fright.

*Emma Pellow (8)*
*Mylor Bridge Primary School*

## IN THE DARK

Dark is at night,
There isn't any light,
What can you see
Hiding behind a tree?
Roofs and chimney pots
Above fires that are hot.
Moon and stars in the sky
That sparkle up high.
Streetlights from afar
And headlights of cars.
Windows glistening far and near
Through which I can peer.
I know why I don't like dark at night
Because it's too light.

*Clare Johnson  (8)*
*Mylor Bridge Primary School*


## CATS

Cats are cuddly
Cats are playful
Cats are scratchy
Cats are soft
Cats are friendly
Cats are funny
Cats are nasty
Cats are nosy
Cats are lonely
Cats are lovely.

*Leanne Curtis  (8)*
*Nine Maidens CP School*

## RABBITS

Rabbits hop.
Rabbits jump.
Rabbits prick their ears.
Rabbits eat the greenest grass.
Wherever it appears.

*Rachel Gray (8)*
*Nine Maidens CP School*


## BUNNY RABBITS

Bunny rabbits have some nasty habits
Like scratching you and kicking.
Some are friendly
Some are good
Some are fond of licking.

*Emma Craythorne (7)*
*Nine Maidens CP School*


## SPACEMAN

I see a spaceman flying
through the atmosphere.
His silver sparkling suit
is getting very hot.
His rocket blasts onto the moon.
The astronaut will be there soon.

*Carl Harvey (7)*
*Nine Maidens CP School*

## DOGS

Dogs eat anything
Bones, chews and dog food

Dogs sleep anywhere
In their bed
Or on the settee

Dogs chase the postman
and the milkman.

I like dogs.

*Ben Page  (8)*
*Nine Maidens CP School*


## BUDGIES

Budgies thin, budgies fat,
Play together have a snack.
Fly around the room all day,
Cheep, cheep is what they say.
Ladders, bells and seeds,
To make them happy,
That is what they need.
They sleep in a cage all through the night,
They are very quiet until it is light.

*Chantelle Goldsworthy  (8)*
*Nine Maidens CP School*

## TWINS

Me and you
both have flu

Me and you
have nothing to do

Me and you
both called Sue

Me and you
both wear blue

Me and you
same, whatever we do.

*Samantha Allen  (8)*
*Nine Maidens CP School*

## PLAYTIME

Playing with my friends
Kicking the ball in the net.
Eating crisps
Chasing each other in a game of 'It'
Hiding around the corner
Sitting, chatting with my friends

And then the
           *Bell!*

*David Hain  (9)*
*Nine Maidens CP School*

## DOGS

Dogs are cheerful,
In the day they are bright,
They always seem to bark
When day turns into night.

When people come near
They bark and growl
When they hear other dogs
They whine and howl.

For their masters
They love to please
Next to backstreet mongrels
They catch lots of fleas.

So don't forget
To give it water and food
Or else your dog won't play
It will become hungry and in a mood.

*Melissa Swain  (8)*
*Nine Maidens CP School*


## THE SPACESHIP

The spaceship zooming around space.
Crashing straight into Neptune.
Smashing into Pluto.
Hitting every planet.
Getting frazzled by the sun.
Being spat through the black hole like a piece
of bubble gum.

*Leigh Makin  (9*
*Nine Maidens CP School*

## WHEN I GO TO BED

When I go to bed at night,
I hear scratching under the stairs,
I think that it might be a ghost,
Or a tiger or a bear,
But I try to think it might be the dog.
That doesn't work
It won't go away.
Suddenly the door opens
I hide under the bed covers
My dad walks in
I'm not afraid anymore.

*Harriet Abrahams  (9)*
*Nine Maidens CP School*


## RABBIT TROUBLE

Rabbits, rabbits with all sorts of habits
Escaping from hutches and digging in holes

Running in tunnels, jumping in meadows
Burrows in fields eating fresh grass

A shot of a gun, and it's gone like a flash.

*Jenny Stocker  (8)*
*Nine Maidens CP School*

## TREES

In winter trees are wet and slimy
Trunks are rough and bumpy
Nearly get blown over in the horrible stormy weather.

In spring the buds have just popped out
People climbing in the huge great trees

In summer when the bright green leaves are out
People sitting in their tree-houses

In autumn, yellow, red and orange leaves fall in
the cold, chilly weather.

*Hannah Mason  (9)*
*Nine Maidens CP School*


## MY LITTLE SISTER

I have a sister called Tanisha
She is short with a cheeky grin
and gappy teeth.
Sometimes I think she is half human
and half hamster,
Because she shreds up paper and leaves
it on the floor.
But I love her really whatever she does.

*Vicky Jane  (10)*
*Perranarworthal CP School*

# MY UNCLE DAVID

My Uncle David is quite thin and has blue eyes
He is married to Claire and will be a dad in July
He is mad on computers especially
boring Star Trek games
He thinks the internet is great
He is on-line all the time

My Uncle David has a green MG
He drives around with a great deal of delight
I think he drives his car too fast
As around he goes selling insurance

My Uncle David wears all the in-things
He likes a good laugh now and then
I like my Uncle David the way he is
Especially when he takes me out.

*Matthew Richards (10)*
*Perranarworthal CP School*


# BOB

I have this friend, his name is Bob
He has a very stressful job
He is 49 years old
His job is to cut down trees
Then he makes logs from these.
He has a weird piano
On it he spent £500.
So if you want to find out more
Go down School Hill and knock on his door.

*Kevin Rogers (10)*
*Perranarworthal CP School*

## OLIVER MY SKINNY LITTLE BROTHER

I have a two-year- old skinny little brother
His name is Oliver.
Oliver's nickname is OJ
He does not have much hair.

OJ is cute and funny
He is a pain some of the time
but sometimes he is good and helpful.
OJ is rude but I still like him even
when he is horrible to me.

Oliver gets mad when I say things
over and over again to him.
He is a fan of Teletubbies
Everyone thinks that OJ is cute but
maybe they are wrong because he is
not very good at home.

*Kirsty Dixon  (10)*
*Perranarworthal CP School*


## OLIVER

My friend Kirsty has a two year old brother
His name is Oliver
His star sign is Libra
He calls her meany
When she is horrible to him
He swears, punches and pinches
And she still loves him!

*Lauren Keeves  (11)*
*Perranarworthal CP School*

## My Friend

I know a kid
He's in my class
He's one of my best friends.
He eats chocolate custard and ice-cream for pudding
For dinner he eats fish fingers and beans.
When I go there I have sausages instead.

I like my friend
Because he likes the same stuff as me.
But he can be a pain because he gets in my way
When we go down hills on our bikes
Because he zooms in front of me
And I fall off
Then he says I'm crazy
Because I do it again.

*Luca Killick  (10)*
*Perranarworthal CP School*


## Jamie Johnson

Jamie Johnson is my rude football coach
He wears silly hats because he is absolutely bald.
He has a hat for when he is happy
He has a hat for when he is sad.
His favourite phrase is
'Come on lads, keep your heads up.'
He often calls me Chrissie Madeley.
He drives very quickly
He wears Saucony trainers
He has holes in his trousers.

*Christopher Madeley  (10)*
*Perranarworthal CP School*

## MY SWIMMING COACH

The tall blonde figure of our fit coach
spurs us on with her supportive words.
'Go, go, go' shouted Liz Burnard
even though I was trying hard,
and like a little water lizard,
went whizzing past the lifeguard.
At the end of the pool she stands
waving us on with her hands.
Watching us doing tumble-turns
making sure we get them right.
If they're not, out we get to do
ten press-ups on the side.
But when we do fine she smiles
and that's a good sign.

*John Hills  (10)*
*Perranarworthal CP School*


## ABÉ A FRIEND IN CLASS!

She has long, blonde hair
Everybody fiddles with it,
She's horse crazy
And has four of her own,
She's got freckles around her nose.
She's kind and almost everybody
Can get on with her,
She's my friend.

*Sofia Killick  (10)*
*Perranarworthal CP School*

## MY WHACKY BEST FRIEND

I have a whacky best friend
who is called Sarah,
She's mad on Aaron Carter
and she reads 'Shout'.
She always says 'Hu'! Charming,'
to me!
She dances and sings
She's talented!
She has a funny laugh like
a hyena howling beneath
a tree.
When she's happy she goes
cock-a-hoop,
She goes a bit weird,
and when she's grumpy,
that means she's sad.
But she's my friend.
My *best, best* friend.

*Katie Savill  (9)*
*Perranarworthal CP School*


## A SISTER

She is my friend's sister called Tanisha
She's four years old and a metre high.
She's forever packing things in bags and crying
because her brother teases her.
Sometimes she is cute, sometimes annoying.
Sometimes she gets a big bag of Barbie dolls
and tips them all over the floor.

*Tom Levick  (10)*
*Perranarworthal CP School*

## THE BEST SECRETARY EVER

Listen, listen what's that sound?
It's Mrs Kemp at the football ground.
Cheering loudly as can be
as Perranwell score number 3.

Monday morning at Perranwell School
Mrs Kemp is looking cool
'Alright me 'andsomes?
How are you?
Got your swimming money, Hugh?'

'Mrs Kemp is that you?
Andrew's got a touch of flu.'
'Thanks for ringing to let us know
It's a busy morning, I've got to go.'

'Mrs Kemp I've hurt my knee.'
'Move your hand and let me see.
That looks nasty, never mind
let's wipe your tears and you'll be fine.'

In the staff room sipping tea is
Mrs Kemp and Mrs Lea.
Saying how they need a rest
from cleaning up the children's mess.

Perranwell school won't be the same
without the sound of Mrs Kemp's name.
We will miss her very much
but we still hope she'll keep in touch.

*Lucy O'Boy  (10)*
*Perranarworthal CP School*

## MY SISTER

I have a sister called Michelle
She's got brown eyes and brown hair
She gets on my nerves by playing on the computer
She's mad on books and horses as well
The horse she loves the most is off the moors
She reads books about horses
Her bookshelf is full of books
You can't get anymore books on it.

*Suzi Brook  (9)*
*Perranarworthal CP School*


## OUR TEACHER

Our teacher is called Mrs Warman
Our teacher likes Arsenal
Our teacher really likes navy blue
Our teacher isn't very good looking
Our teacher is a real bossy boots
Our teacher uses Nivea
Our teacher likes sport
Our teacher is quite fun
Our teacher always wears scarves.

*Adam Laskey  (11)*
*Perranarworthal CP School*


## MUM

She is always busy
She is very independent,
She has a great personality
And she loves horses.

She has the odd mood
And she often gets in a temper
But she is my mum and I love her.

*Abé Struggles  (11)*
*Perranarworthal CP School*

## MY UNCLE JOHN

My Uncle John has got a nose as pointy
as the Eiffel Tower,
I am always getting up his nose,
Until he decides to chase me.

He is always showing off because,
He is unbeatable on Age of Empires.

His dog, Sam, is brilliant at football,
But we beat Sam at playing ball.

His other dog is called Tiger,
Tiger is a little whippersnapper,
Who runs and barks around your feet.

His fiancée, our nearly Auntie Val,
Comes from Ireland,
And has a proper Irish accent.

I would like to see my Uncle John
right now!
I really like my Uncle John, he is a
really good pal.

*Tom Hastings  (10)}*
*Perranarworthal CP School*

## MY BRO CHRIS

My brother is so annoying,
He tells on everything,
He gets away with everything.

My brother is so annoying,
With a good mood,
And a bad mood.

My brother is okay,
His body is plump and short,
His hair is spiky and short.

(*Umm!*) My brother is the best,
The best in the world ever,
I'm not exactly sure,
But I think I will like him . . .
. . . *For ever!*

*Matthew Clements  (11)*
*Perranarworthal CP School*


## LIZZIE!

She likes to say, 'Out the way, Lizzie coming through.'
She is funny, strange and daft all in one but still kind.
She is one of my best friends.
I like her because of her naughty face and her cheesy grin.
She is very kind to me and quite clever.
She has short, brown hair,
And her freckles seem to have been pecked in by woodpeckers.

*Florence Lawson  (10)*
*Perranarworthal CP School*

## MY BEST FRIEND

She's cool, she's fun, she's one of a kind
She's good and a friend of mine.
      She likes to . . .
Dance and sing and play, she likes her
horses Red and Jess
      She's in love with . . .
Leonardo di Caprio, Titanic the film
and the main thing Aaron Carter.
We love him, we sing and dance to
      his songs! We have a lot of things
      in common.

We sleep over at each other's houses
and beautify each other reading all
the mags in sight.
Her favourite mags are 'Smash Hits' and 'TV Hits'.

The main phrase you
hear us say is talking American
and Australian.
      She has . . .
Long, dark brown hair, brown eyes, long face,
pointy nose, square jaw and size four feet.
Like me.

*Sarah Bottono  (9)*
*Perranarworthal CP School*

## MY SISTER HOPE

Hope is my little four year old sister,
She tries to do head-over-heels but
they end up going wrong!
Sometimes she is kind to me but
sometimes she is horrid,
she has a cute smile and wears it every day,
she gets into tantrums when Dad winds her up,
I like her a lot even when she is mean,
she calls me a pile of flubber when I do headstands.

*Helen Keeves (9)*
*Perranarworthal CP School*




## MEGAN (MY SISTER)

My sister looks like an angel,
But she's the toddler from hell,
She raids my bedroom looking for make-up,
She tips nail varnish all over the carpets,
And wastes loads of lipstick by putting it on the walls.
And I get the blame for leaving my make-up out.
She's got blonde curly hair and blue eyes
That you can swim in.
Everyone says she's so cute . . .
But you don't know her like I do!

*Lizzie Job (10)*
*Perranarworthal CP School*

## MRS KEMP

At the football match she'll shout and scream,
cheering on her favourite team.
Selling teas and drinks in a can,
she is Perranwell's number one fan.

Mrs Kemp is football mad,
she's been watching it since her boy was a lad.
Perranwell, Perranwell is her cheer,
she hopes they'll win the cup this year!

She's been school sec for 30 years,
putting plasters on cuts and wiping away tears.
'Alright my love?' you hear her say,
'Come on kids, swimming money today.'

Every Monday she goes out prancing,
shaking her legs while she's line dancing.
It's the new dance that's all the rage,
she shows up kids half her age.

Eyes as blue as the deep blue sea,
she's always happy. Tall as a tree.
Mrs Kemp has helped us all through the years
So let's give her . . . *three big cheers!*

*Mark Stephenson & Karl Martin (9)*
*Perranarworthal CP School*

## MY NAN

My nan
Lives in a bungalow on Carron Downs.
My nan goes shopping on Tuesdays
When she gets home she's always broke
Because she buys us lots of sweets and treats!
I like my nan for that.

My nan is old and wrinkly
Like your fingers when you've just come out of the bath.
My nan has got false teeth
And a scar on her chest
Which is red and purple.

My nan likes sewing
She does it as a job and a hobby.
My nan goes line dancing
As her other hobby
With my Auntie Dor on Friday nights.

My nan likes cooking.
She cooks us chips on Tuesdays.
At Christmas she always makes a Christmas cake.
She likes making teacakes
She always sends one home for my dad.

*Lauren Howell 10)*
*Perranarworthal CP School*

## INFINITY AND BEYOND

To infinity and beyond
A famous actor said.
But does he think of what it means
And start to scratch his head?

But what's beyond infinity?
Some scientists say nothing.
But if nothing's beyond infinity
Then what's beyond the nothing?

Some scientists say space goes on for ever
And it does never end.
Some say it's a speck in a goldfish bowl
And some say it's a marble at the glass ball end.

Aliens are out there
On Venus, Pluto and Mars.
Aliens the size of us
And some the size of stars.

We may think aliens look strange
But we have found no evidence.
They may think that we look strange
Running around like ants.

But none of this we know for sure
So the scientists say.
But just between you and me
The aliens have come to stay.

So this is why we wonder
What's lurking in the starry pond?
But what we should be thinking,
Is, what's in infinity and beyond?

*Matthew Ronchetti (10)*
*Quethiock Voluntary Aided CE Primary School*

## MY FRIEND

He is my oaken staff on my dusty way.
He is my shield, he will always protect me.
He is the friend who will never forget me.
He is the neighbour that is never away.
If I am the gate, then he is the post.
He is there when I need him the most.
He is an asset, never a burden.
He will always listen, never turn a deaf ear.
I never need wish for him, he is always here.
He is more reliable than anyone could know.
He does not care if I am bad at sport.
He does not care if my IQ is nought.
He is not a professor, a teacher of skills.
He is not a falcon, soaring on high.
But none of that helps to stop my cry.
He is my shadow, always by my side.
He is the light at the end of the tunnel.
He is kind, good, trustworthy and loyal.
He is -
My friend.

*Katherine Healey (11)*
*Quethiock Voluntary Aided CE Primary School*


## THE WEATHER

You should never underestimate the weather,
It can change from minute to minute,
One minute it is sunny,
The next it could be raining.
The weather is a very strong and powerful thing,
Lightning could kill you instantly.
Imagine the idea of controlling the weather!
If we wanted a nice sunny day we could have one or two
                                        or whatever!

Everyone has a favourite weather.
The farmers would want rain for their crops to grow,
Children would want sunshine to play at the seaside,
Every living thing needs a certain amount of rain,
And nature usually does a good job of it.
Do we need to interfere with the weather?
I'm happy with it, aren't you?

*Matthew Tamblyn  (11)*
*Quethiock Voluntary Aided CE Primary School*

## THE WIND

Moving the waves on the beach.
Gentle breezes,
Terrible hurricanes,
Trees moving gently.
Swaying,
Peacefully.
Such force and power,
North against South,
Fighting for ever.
Never stop.
Terror!
We fall on our feet in mercy.
Destroying.
Then it calms.
Into a summer breeze.
Gently against our skin
Softly,
And then it stops.
With the sun burning our skin.
Hurricanes!
Tornadoes!

*Wendy Anne Pollard  (11)*
*Quethiock Voluntary Aided CE Primary School*

# A MAN A SOLDIER A GUN

I look out of my window and see a heartbreaking sight.
A man
A soldier
A gun
I hope this bullet will not go through my window
Like the last time.
*Bang!*
*Bang!*
*Bang!*
Oh no, what was that?
It was a gun and it sounded so near.
I walked to the stairs
And at the foot of the stairs
I saw my father.
My dead father.
My mother was crying beside him.
Now I know why that gun sounded so near.

*Dee-Anne Kate Thomas  (10)*
*Quethiock Voluntary Aided CE Primary School*


# COSMIC

Spaceships twirling in the sky,
Whizzing, whizzing, like a butterfly
See the engine roaring
See the moon flying by
Look I can fly,
In the dark sky
See him do loop the loop,
See the lights flashing by
See the fire when it blasts
            *5 4 3 2 1*

We have ignition!
If you see the moon
It will soon be your doom
The moon in the black night
See the sun in the bright light
The only light is the earth
*Down, down,* below
The moon says 'Goodbye'
Then the sun pops up and says 'Hi.'

*Richard Day  (10)*
*Quethiock Voluntary Aided CE Primary School*


## VOLCANOES

Lava running down the mountainside,
Boiling rock rushing through crevices.
Molten rock bubbling ferociously,
Steam whooshing into the sky.

Vibrant red pouring down,
Ash spurting in the air.
Orange lava flowing slowly,
Greatest power on earth.

Enhancing the earth's magical colours.
So little warning but
            Massive destruction.
            Unstoppable.

*Peter Geall  (10)*
*Quethiock Voluntary Aided CE Primary School*

# FIRE

Flames rising high into the sky,
Spirits dancing with the smoke.
Orange, yellow, blue.
Merging together to make an explosion of . . .
Love, faith, joy,
Warmth reaching into every corner of my heart,
Hope, loyalty, freedom,
Smoke enclosing me in a spiral,
Lifting my thoughts to
The homeless,
The poor,
The weak,
How can I help?
Life isn't fair!
Why is it like this?
I don't understand,
Suffering.
Pain,
Ashes are all that are left now,
Not such a pretty sight as before.

*Briony Primrose Bradbeer (11)*
*Quethiock Voluntary Aided CE Primary School*


# COSMIC - MY DOG

Someone to welcome me when I come home
He's a loyal playful pup
With a patch by his ear and a snip of a nose
He's the only friend I've got.

We play in the garden with his favourite toy
He eats from a round red pot
He sleeps by the fire in a cosy basket
He's the only friend I've got.

He wakes up in the morning
And barks to wake me up
We snuggle up on the sofa
He's the only friend I've got.

When I take him for a walk
He bounds off on the lead
But I know he won't forget
That I'm the friend he's got.

*Amy Louise Jopling (10)*
*Quethiock Voluntary Aided CE Primary School*


## STRANGE NEIGHBOURS

There are some strange neighbours living next door.
They always pass by without saying a word.
They never say hello.
They never say goodbye.
What strange, strange neighbours!

They have a strange dog,
That doesn't wag its tail.
It's afraid of cats.
It doesn't like bats.
What a strange, strange dog!

They have a strange cat,
That's not afraid of dogs.
He doesn't drink milk.
What a strange, strange cat!

There are some strange neighbours living next door.
They have a strange cat.
They have a strange dog.
What strange, strange, neighbours.

*David Henwood (10)*
*Quethiock Voluntary Aided CE Primary School*

## MONDAY MORNING

Waking up with dreary eyes,
Looking up into the skies,
Thinking, do I have to get up?
And then feed my dog's new pup?
Monday morning's such a bore,
Does it have to happen anymore?

Once I've got up from my bed,
I rub my eyes and then my head.
I go over to my pile of clothes,
Which one shall I pick of those?
Maybe it will be my grey skirt?
Or perhaps my neat white shirt?

Next I shall run down the stairs,
Clomping like a herd of mares.
With spoon in hand I gulp and slurp,
My breakfast's gone in one big burp!
Monday mornings, such a bore,
Does it have to happen anymore?

I pick up my brush, for my hair is tangled,
When I'm finished brushing it doesn't look mangled.
I quickly grab my bag and run down the road,
And to my amazement I see a squashed toad!
Oh no! The time, now the Demon Headmaster,
Next time will make me go even faster.

*I'm late!*

**Colette Gregory  (10)**
**Quethiock Voluntary Aided CE Primary School**

## VISIT TO SPACE

Up, up, up
until you reach the sky.

I eye the bright silver stars shining in the sky.
I think how exciting it would be to ride along the sky
on the tail of a silver comet.

*Zoom, boom, whizz,* as we whizz past Saturn
*Zoom, boom, whizz,* as we whizz past Neptune.

At last we land on Mars. As we meet three aliens,
they crown me Queen of Mars and we zoom back to Earth
in a shower of silver sparks.

*Emma Yeo  (9)*
*St Catherine's CE School, Launceston*


## LIFT OFF

*5, 4, 3, 2, 1,* Off the rocket goes, into outer space,
It zoom off at such a wonderful pace,

Off to another place.
*Zoom!* There it goes! *Zoom!*
Off it goes, *boom, boom, boom*!
I wonder where it's going? Maybe to the moon?
What's going on up there? *Bang! Clang! Crash!*
Looks like a big bash! *Clash*!

*Lucy Littlejohns  (9)*
*St Catherine's CE School, Launceston*

## I WENT TO SPACE

I looked at the world through the moon's eyes
It was quite beautiful.
And had changed in size,
But then I zoomed off
Until all the cities and countries
Had faded from sight.
I whizzed right away from the moon's milky white light
I zoomed past Mars, Jupiter, Mercury.
So, mum, if you are missing me
I hope to be back in time for tea.

*Ruth Griffiths  (9)*
*St Catherine's CE School, Launceston*


## ROCKET INTO SPACE

*Zoom* goes the rocket into space.
When you get out and walk into the place,
you run back to the rocket when you see a funny face,
you leave when you hear your friend calling,
'Help, help me.'
You zoom back, grab her, pull her into the rocket.
You go home, have tea and go to bed
with a cup of cocoa.

*Rebecca Brown  (8)*
*St Catherine's CE School, Launceston*

## I'M NOT SURE

Space is a black sky,
full of planets,
full of stars
full of comets
full of aliens . . .
I'm not sure.

Space is a black sky,
Why it's black, I'm not sure why,
I saw a rocket taking off,
I'm sure I'd be better off,
Staying home instead,
Curled up in bed!

*Rebecca Langsford (8)*
*St Catherine's CE School, Launceston*


## WHEN I SAW A SPACESHIP

In the dark, dark sky I saw a spaceship fly,
Past the moon, past the stars, it really did fly.
Past my bedroom and shed, it landed in
My garden and that was the end of that.

*Tom Conie (9)*
*St Catherine's CE School, Launceston*

## AQUA CITY

I'm going on holiday this year
To Majorca!
I've been there twice before.
I'm looking forward to Aqua City.
The big water slide
*Kamikaze!*
It's a straight drop!
My dad said,
'If you go down there, I'll give you a fiver.'
I went down,
But he didn't give me it!
The Black Hole,
It goes round and round and round and round
And you get really *dizzy,*
And when you reach the bottom,
The rubber ring tips you *upside down!*

*Ben Atherton  (10)*
*St Columb Major CP School*


## MY BED

It's as cosy as cuddling a dog,
It's as warm as a fire,
It's as bouncy as a trampoline,
I could stay in it for ever,
My bed!
The duvet is as thick as a garden wall,
The pillow is as soft as a puppy,
The sheets are like envelopes that I slip inside,
Protecting me from life outside.

*Tom Davey  (10)*
*St Columb Major CP School*

## CATS
*(In memory of Chip, killed shortly after
this poem was written)*

Three cats,
Chip, Dale and Molly.
They sit there looking around,
Out of the cat flap.
Jump about,
And back again!
Fluffy little things.
They play and jump and pounce about,
But they never want to hurt you.
They sit there and purr,
Give you kisses
Now and again!
They play with all their might,
*I love them!*
And they love me.
We're all one family.
They bite and claw,
Hiss and wag their tails, long and short.
They seem to sleep at day or night,
But everything they do
is all right by me.

*Rachelle Forrest  (10)*
*St Columb Major CP School*

## BABY BROTHERS

I love my brother, Matthew,
Even if he's annoying,
He's cute and cuddly,
And loads of fun.
He tells me his problems,
By going ga ga ga ga,
Even though he can't talk,
But he's still my little brother.
I love him,
He's cute and cuddly like a
Teddy bear.
He watches the telly,
He watches my hands,
His fingers are like small diamonds,
His eyes are like blue gems,
He's like a jewel,
A shining star in my *life!*

*Gemma Hall  (10)*
*St Columb Major CP School*


## MY PUPPY

Zippy,
Chews up the carpet,
Bites my fingers and toes.
He's got a sweet-smelling scent and  . . .
A little button nose.

We call him Mr Mole for short,
I don't know why!
Zippy's going to be put down soon and
I'm going to cry!

He's a rascal and
He is afraid of the car.
Chloe the mum is a sweetie,
Zippy is as black as tar.

I love my lovely Mr Mole,
A friendly soul is he,
Zippy is so silly,
A friend he is to me.

*Briony Chapman  (10)*
*St Columb Major CP School*


## PRINCE

Walking my dog
Is a muddy experience!
But when I get home
I have a lovely warm bath
My dog is like royalty
No wonder he is called Prince!
Sasha my other dog
Playfights with Prince.
Prince once bit off Sasha's ear,
The vet couldn't stitch it back on!
Prince even bites our hosepipe!
When my dad turned it on,
Water showered over him from the tiny holes.
I give Prince shoulder rides,
He's really heavy!
He's scared of horses
And of my cat, Puss-Puss!
Prince is a darling,
My mum doesn't think that, though.
Would you?

*Laura J Dolan  (10)*
*St Columb Major CP School*

## GIZZMO

My dog,
Cute brown eyes,
Floppy dangling down ears,
We play a lot together,
He likes chewing insoles out of shoes,
Especially my dad's,
I feel sorry
When he gets a smack,
On the nose
For being so naughty!
He's got a black nose
With a pink spot,
His tail curls upwards,
And waggles a lot.
What else does he do?
Digs holes, drinks cups of tea,
Barks at visitors,
He's my dog,
*I love him!*

*Janine Lawer  (10)*
*St Columb Major CP School*


## HORSE MAD

Brill I got him for Christmas,
His name is Coco.
We went to a field,
And a Christmas present was there for me!
He bolts four times,
I come off!

I get back on.
He doesn't worry me,
He's only little,
And such a sweet face,
I had a gallop he was fine,
He did what I wanted.

He's so sweet, he fills me with glee.

*Laura Perry  (11)*
*St Columb Major CP School*

## GETTING MY OWN BACK

My sister is a pain,
hitting me, if she's annoyed with my dad
for some reason.
She lies about me too,
I am like her stress doll.
One incident stands out in my recent memory,
'I mean, fair enough I hit her, but I didn't
hit her first.'
'Did too.'
'Did not.'
'Did too.'
'Did not!'

Oh how I'd like to get my own back on her,
for being such a pain.
Strapping her to a rocket and sending her
to the moon seems a bit drastic.
'Cos she's all right,
in a mysterious kind of way.

*Simon Riley  (9)*
*St Columb Major CP School*

## MY PARENTS

Mum and dad, they're the best parents ever.
Mum works at school all day.
Then every other day at night she's at the Co-op working.
I'm in bed by the time she gets home!
Dad works in Padstow from 6am to 5pm,
He's tired by the time I see him.
They need to work to give me
And my brothers
Luxuries like school camp.
Me and dad are going on the Camel Trail on Saturday,
I finally get to spend some hours with him.
Mum helps me with my homework,
They both comfort me when I am down,
I love my mum and dad so much,
I will never let them go!

*Helen Jones  (10)*
*St Columb Major CP School*


## SMELLY PIGS

A pink hairy, smelly, snorting,
ugly, chubby pig,
They make me vomit,
Rolling in mud,
Eating slops from last Sunday's roast,
Piglets turning into fat flabby fools.
It's hard for them to walk
Carrying a million tons of junk food.
If the pig was my mum I could eat
As much junk food as possible!
Just like my brother!

*Kimberly Bazeley  (10)*
*St Columb Major CP School*

## THE BRIT AWARDS 1998

Fireworks, the big screen,
Ladies and gentlemen,
The Brit Awards 1998.
Scary Baby, Ginger, Sporty and Posh,
The Spice Girls!
Ginger Spice wrapped in the Union Jack,
As we try to prove Britain is the best in pop music.
For most of us it's the closest we get to meeting the stars.
When they gather together,
And try to win the best awards,
A night of glamour,
Well,
Maybe not for us!
And the winner is . . .
*Me!*
For staying up to watch it!

*Vicky Tremain (11)*
*St Columb Major CP School*


## FRIENDS

Friends are what get you through life.
Always standing by your side.
Kind and helpful,
Smiling,
Laughing,
Jumping,
Skipping.
At school and at home they are always around.
To race, to play with and to have a laugh.

*Clare Jenkin (9)*
*St Columb Major CP School*

## PEST OF A DOG

My puppy Cassie
chews my cuddly pig!
She pinches my mini eggs.
She steals all the Belgian chocolates at Christmas.

Despite all these things,
she wants us to feel sorry for her!
She plays tug-of-war with Jessie,
her little sister, using *my* bands.
She pulls out all the plastic bags from
the top shelf down!
She jumps over the hedge
and has us run after her.
She tips the food bowl over
and the drinks' bowl too for that matter.
She rips the potato bag open
and starts to eat them.

She rips our underwear up,
but the less said about that the better!
At the end of the day she is a darling.
What would I do without her?

*Katie Varcoe (10)*
*St Columb Major CP School*

## BALLOONS

I often go down to Truro.
I see a man with all sorts of balloons.
I think, how come he doesn't fly away?
Balloons just fly away up, up into the sky,
they are like rainbows all different types
of colours just waiting to pop!
I jump about trying to catch them in
their group as the multicoloured blobs
fly away into space.
They will fly to space now, never
to be seen again unless  . . .
*The aliens see them!*

*Laura Davies  (9)*
*St Columb Major CP School*

## A BEST FRIEND

I have got a best friend
the most treasured person you could have
Always there to help you
cheer you up when you're down and blue
When we have a fall out
yes, it is a fuss
but we get back together again
We are here
We are us.

*Jane Wood  (10)*
*St Columb Major CP School*

## THREE WHIPPETS!

Three whippets,
Nobby, Jed and Hardee.
There were four
But Charlie died.
Nobby is a pain,
He nicks my things
And sprays ink everywhere
When he bites my cartridges.
Jed bites my grandad's hand and when he goes for walkies
He nibbles his ankles.
Hardee's got really sharp teeth,
He's only a puppy.
Jed's a racer
At Cullompton whippet racing.
He is two years old.
I've won five trophies
All with Jed.
He's top dog, ya know
Because he is the only dog there, the rest are bitches.
Nobby is learning,
But Hardee is too young yet.

*Rebecca Shephard  (10)*
*St Columb Major CP School*

# THE SEA

Under the vast ocean
a thousand rainbow fish dance
Escaping bubbles
rise up from
coral reefs
Dolphins play
whilst upon thesurface
near the shore,
palm trees sway
in the summer breeze.
Coconuts fall
onto the golden sands.
Breaking the waters
a dolphin flips up
splashing sightseers
streamlining through the water
sandy rainbow fish scurrying.

*Tessa Crawford  (10)*
*St Columb Major CP School*

## KAWASAKI

Kawasaki,
80cc of throbbing power!
Revving and revving.
At the old train track,
If my brother has time,
It's on a Sunday.
He watches.
I ride.
I love my Kawasaki.
Soft seat,
Spring suspension.
Cosy throttle.
And away I go for a ride.
*Away I go.*
When I fall,
I get back on again.
I will not get hurt.
I ride like a *little lunatic*
And then in the shed it goes.

*Aaron Rundle  (10)*
*St Columb Major CP School*

## SPELLINGS

I am not very good
*At spellings!*
I have two dictionaries
But what use are they
When you can't spell?
My friend Kristin thinks this
as well.
We always ask Laura
Because she's good at them.
My teacher gave me a spellmaster
but in an hour and a half I ran
the batteries out.
Last week I got all my spellings
right in the test.
But they were very easy.
*Everybody got them right!*
I'll keep trying
And then one day I'll be
a gud spelr!

**Gemma Davis (10)**
**St Columb Major CP School**

## MUSIC

Cymbals clashing,
Drums beating,
CDs whizzing as they play.
Gentle piano playing,
Noisy, flashing discos.
Bells jingle as they ring,
Shakers clatter when being shaken.
Singing, laughing, dances too.
Tambourines clashing and jingling for me.
I enjoy playing the piano,
                    Gentle, wild, playful music too.
Guitars playing, drums banging,
Cymbals clashing, bells ringing.
Gentle, loving music, loud, wild music.
Slow tunes, fast tunes,
Music of all types.
I wouldn't know what to do without music.

*Alice Brenton  (9)*
*St Columb Major CP School*


## THE SEA

The sea roars like a lion
Whooshes like the wind.
It rages like an angry giant.
The sea is calm like a sleeping baby.
No sound comes from its depths.
It is as quiet as a mouse.

*Craig James  (11)*
*St Erme With Trispen CP School, Truro*

## WEATHER

It's raining, it's raining
I hope that it will brighten up or I
will start to cry
but what do you think?
I am getting very scared now,
because it's getting very windy now.

Now it is raining and hailing very hard
the weather is getting very fierce
so I am very scared.

It is blowing up for a thunderstorm
so thunder is going to come
bang, bang it goes
and then the lightning comes
flash, flash it goes.

Here comes a tornado, a big swirling wind
'Down to the basement,' my mum calls
'But first we must open all of the windows
and when it's blown over we'll go to the
city hall.'

But now the weather is very fierce
and I hope that it will blow
over soon, for I will be relieved.

*Zoe Rawicki  (10)*
*St Erme With Trispen CP School, Truro*

## SPOILT CHILD

I beat my fists of wind and rain,
Hard against your window-pane,
I'm angry with your rays of sun,
Now is my time for fierce fun,
I feel blustery, I feel wild,
I am the twisted spoilt child.

       My helter-skelter ride of biting,
       Wind and rain and jagged lightning,
       I'll storm around in a screaming fight,
       I'll bring the clouds to black out your light,
       I won't be meek, I won't be mild,
       I am the twisted spoilt child.

You can't calm or quieten me down,
You can't stop my wintry frown,
You can't stop my shapeless form,
Here I am the spoilt storm,
I am angry, I am riled,
I *am* the twisted spoilt child.

*Chloe Hart  (10)*
*St Erme With Trispen CP School, Truro*


## THERE IS AN OLD MAN I KNOW

There is an old man I know
Who lives in the forest glade
He waves his bony fingers
To me as I walk through the forest glade

There is an old man I know
Who rocks on his rocking chair
Rocking with a silky ginger cat
Asleep on his lap

There is an old man I know
Who I found lying in bed one day
I asked what was wrong
And he whispered to me
'I'm dying, I'm dying
Take Ginger, take Ginger
And please look after her'
I wept for him
Then took Ginger home with me.

*Nicola Hawke  (10)*
*St Erme With Trispen CP School, Truro*

# THE TIDAL WAVE

He builds up like a weightlifter, in silence and
with power.
And gathering water from below with unseen hands
he moulds and shapes his mighty wall.
When time is ripe and building done, this is when
the danger comes.
He smashes over the waves below him, like toys
thrown across a floor.
To avoid him is impossible, he will get you in
the end.
When land is reached and damage done, and peace
returns once more.
Be glad he only came to play, and stopped so soon
and went away.
Remember him always, with respect and never turn
your back, he could just be waiting for another
surprise attack.

*Kieran Cooper  (10)*
*St Erme With Trispen CP School, Truro*

## WIND

He is a roaring lion
Raging across the sky
He crashes down trees
Breaks into houses
And sets the babies crying
He takes away hats
And umbrellas too
Blows down telephone wires
And in his anger just for luck
He will blow off a chimney pot
But his power can never last
For the sun will come shining through
Who could this be?
Nobody but
*The wind.*

*Jen Saywell  (9)*
*St Erme With Trispen CP School, Truro*


## FRIENDS

Make a new friend happy
but don't make an old friend sad
then you won't have a friend
you'll have *friends*.

Don't bring up bad things
that make you feel sad
put the bad memories
at the bottom of the sea!
But don't forget to put up a
*no* fishing sign
then you won't hurt your mates!

*Freya Coglan  (11)*
*St Erme With Trispen CP School, Truro*

## ANNOYING PEOPLE GOING ON

'Sit down, shut up,
Get on with your work.'
That's the teachers going on
and on and on.

'Get up, get ready for school.'
That's my mum going on
and on and on.

I wish they'd shut up
and leave me alone
and let me sleep on a
bit more.

*Lisa Reeks  (10)*
*St Erme With Trispen CP School, Truro*

## AT THE BEACH

I suck them up and spit them out,
I rip them up and smash them down,
Step on them and crush them flat;
Blowing, I fight him in the storm.

I whoosh and call for my friends,
Tornado, hurricane and all;
We go out and vandalise property
Not ours but the world's . . .
. . .*I am a tidal wave!*

*Thomas Connell  (10)*
*St Erme With Trispen CP School, Truro*

## THE TREES ARE LIKE . . .

The trees are like . . .
An old man
Who sighs in the wind.

The trees are like . . .
An old man
With sore arthritic hands.

The trees are like . . .
An old man
Crying all the time.

The trees are like . . .
An old man
With big bulging hair.

The trees are like . . .
An old man
With hard skin around his body.

The trees are like . . .
An old man
Who weeps because of his age.

*Aimie Cole  (11)*
*St Erme With Trispen CP School, Truro*

## THE RAIN-MAKER

He keeps his jewels in a room
Very dark and damp,
And when he's in the doom and gloom
He will shout and stamp.

His jewels fly out of his palace
And pour down to the lands,
He doesn't care about his malice
Rain spilling from his hands.

If he looks as black as thunder
He will send a storm,
We can only watch and wonder
While his tricks he does perform.

His jewels dissolve into puddles
When they hit the ground,
Everyone goes round in huddles
Feet make a splashing sound.

Suddenly he goes to sleep
And then disappears,
All the other rain-makers weep
With their enormous tears.

*Bethany Key  (11)*
*St Erme With Trispen CP School, Truro*

## SOMETHING OR SOMEONE

There it blows past my ears
Makes me shiver in my shoes
And it calls me by my name
It's as if it sings to me
A song that no one sings.

I run from room to room
In the great haunted house
At the end of the road
Thinking I should have never come here!
It was but a dare.

I screamed as I saw it
It saw my fear
With a great big black tunic
Staring at my face.

I know that they would tease me
I know that I would cry
But anything's better than here -
For it's death that runs past my ear.

*Danielle Penny  (10)*
*St Erme With Trispen CP School, Truro*


## MY GRAN

Sometimes my gran sleeps in her chair,
But most of the time she just wants to stare.
My gran likes the colour red,
She said.

When I go in the house, gran says to me,
'Get out of the house if you're ever unhappy.'
'Where is that cat who sits on the bed?'
She said.

'Come on,' my gran says to me,
as we walk to the cafe.
'Now if you don't eat this I will tip it on
your head.'
She said.

'Be quiet now, it's very late.'
'It's been a very important date.'
'Come on you ratbag, it's time for bed.'
She said.

*Laura Jones (10)*
*St Erme With Trispen CP School, Truro*


## THE AFRICAN PLAINS

The cheetah sprints after his prey.
A speeding Ferrari
flashes by the lioness coiled
like a spring waiting to pounce
on a wild wart-hog, always sniffing,
fat as a barrel of beer.
Above, an eagle, king of the sky
is a hovering cloud
watching the motionless crocodile lying
like a fallen log in the turbid water,
muddied by the stampeding
midnight express of wildebeests.
Much slower, the plodding elephants
rumble like rolling boulders.
Disturb herds of zebra who unravel
like an endless roll of stripy wallpaper
across the dry, grassy plain.

*Tom Somers (11)*
*St Hilary CP School, Truro*

## DEATH IS A VULTURE

Death is a vulture
Its wings outstretched
Like a flowing cape
Blotting out the daylight
Its head a swivelling radar with
Beady eyes as black as night
Bony talons
Like thorny twigs
It hovers nearby
Always alert
Stalking
Slowly closing in
Silently, swooping down
Like a parachute
Falling to the earth below
It pounces upon its helpless prey
Opening its talons
Onto a world of everlasting
Darkness.

*Kate Hamilton  (10)*
*St Hilary CP School, Truro*


## MY MIND

My mind is a vacuum cleaner,
It sucks up all the facts,
The only trouble is,
It can't handle the important things,
It just bags the rubbish.

When the important bits reach my brain,
They just pass straight through,
Info goes in one ear and out the other,
Some never even reaches my brain at all,
So all in all,
I'm as daft as a brush!

*William Prior  (11)*
*St Hilary CP School, Truro*


## EAGLE

The eagle is an arrow,
Shooting through the clouds,
Silently but quickly
He races through the sky.

As powerful as a lion,
He is king of the air,
All the creatures fear him
On the earth below.

His golden wings glowing
In the brightness of the sun,
Shining like a star,
In the darkness of the clouds.

Talons sharp as knives,
Eyes that see so far,
His beak is a razor
Deadly to his prey.

Gaining on his target,
No mercy he will show,
When he finds his prey
On the ground below.

*Viv Ziar  (10)*
*St Hilary CP School, Truro*

## BULLDOZER

The bulldozer like a huge, meaty buffalo
Crashes into the empty house
With an ear-bursting clatter.
Jogging into walls,
Using its muscle
To power through the bricks.

Rubble dust drifting on the wind
Obscures my view of the beast
As it paws the ground
Snorting exhaust fumes
Ready to charge again.

The last remaining wall
Smashed to smithereens
With animal ferocity.
Splinters of wood and glass
Are hoofed aside
As it makes its new home.

*Mark Hammond (11)*
*St Hilary CP School, Truro*


## THE CROW

The crow caws, shrieking
Like an engine raring to go,
While the pilot, a tiny speck
Within the black, cockpit eyes
Checks the feathers,
A cargo of passengers
Ready to carry on extending wings
Its fuselage
Across a blue, cloudless sky.

*Maree Smith (10)*
*St Hilary CP School, Truro*

# THE WOLF WIND

Like a wolf howling, growling, snarling, biting, barking.
It prowls around the house trying to find a way in.
It scratches the door, it claws at the window,
trying to find a way that isn't barred or bolted.
It moans, groans, whines and wheezes,
circling nearer, nearer, tightening the trap.
It coughs and screams and sneezes.
The sounds are eerie and frightening.
I cannot sleep, I lie listening
to the wind.

*Katie Scrase  (10)*
*St Hilary CP School, Truro*


# VOLCANO

The volcano, a huge doughnut
oozing red hot jam
in a river of red flames.
Sensational reds and oranges
like a coal effect fire,
glow warmly.
Molten rock, like blood
gushes from the wound
forming a flaming hot lake
of spilt milk.
An eruption booms, like a clap of thunder,
lava escapes, just one thing on its mind,
*freedom!*

*Emma Williams  (10)*
*St Hilary CP School, Truro*

## THE SEA

The sea a clambering cat,
Crawling across the sea bed,
His glimmering teeth surface as white, frothy waves,
And sharp, pointed claws scramble to the shore,
Where the sands are like gold pennies,
The waves embrace the brown, slimy rocks
Where moonlight reflects like silver foil
Embedded in the sea.

The buttered sun lays upon the earth,
The sea settles,
The cat's asleep
And purrs as boats trundle above,
As the cat lays along the land!

*Briony Berryman  (10)*
*St Hilary CP School, Truro*


## THE ICE-CREAM

Melting in the glistening sunshine,
Like a candle burning in a room,
Oozing down the crispy golden wafer,
The wax rolls down in drips.

The ice-cream is expiring,
A pink tongue licks it away,
The candle's tongue of flame
Meanwhile flickers in the wind.

Slipping through the fingers,
Ice-cream tumbles to the floor,
The candle has extinguished,
And fallen to its end.

*Holly Bowden  (10)*
*St Hilary CP School, Truro*

## THE SECURITY DOG

Eyes like black marbles
A small hairy beast
With ivory toothpick teeth
Little black leather on his feet
Patches holding tiny bony claws
His fur all spiky as a cactus leaf
Quivers and waits.

Little pixie ears stand on his head
Like two upright soldiers
Standing on guard
Spitting mad
What a little beast!
Like a starting pistol to a race
The ivories are out, what takes place?
The postman's here!

Yorkshire pudding does his best
Tugging and pulling, doing his job
An ox he is not,
But guard dog (or so he thinks).

So walk fast down our path
In case he has not been fed
But if you are very lucky
He will be asleep in his bed.

*Louise Hardcastle (10)*
*St Hilary CP School, Truro*

## THE ROSE

The rose is a heart,
Pumping sprigs of blossom into all our lives,
Its stem is a cactus
With a prickly throat,
Giving pain when touched,
But contented, not harmed.

It grows in mysterious ways,
Crawling slowly up and up,
Swirling, creeping, curving round,
Expanding in and out.
Petals scarlet as the blood inside.

When it comes to a halt,
Things don't look so good,
It gives as much as it can,
Until its final day.

*Tracy Kessell (10)*
*St Hilary CP School, Truro*


## THE RABBIT

I have a bouncy rabbit
with fur as fluffy as cotton wool
and white as snow.
His eyes sparkle like stars up in the sky,
and his nose is shaped like a triangle and very, very dry.
His ears are long like corn that grows in the field,
and when you go to cuddle him he is very still.
My rabbit is a friendly chap who likes to sit on your lap.

*Stephanie Lawrence (11)*
*St Hilary CP School, Truro*

## CHEETAH

Bolting with the wind
like a shot from a gun
fired across the dry plains.
Dodging and gliding over rocks and plants,
it pinpoints a deer,
speeding like a bullet
it pursues and
hits its target.
Drags back his prey
and hangs it from a tree.
The prize of life.

*Ben Walker  (11)*
*St Hilary CP School, Truro*


## CHEETAH

A cheetah is like the sea
Fascinating to watch
Graceful and powerful
Creeping through the long grass
It leaps out
Pounces from nowhere
Like a silent current
Whose waves crash in
With white teeth
Clawing and knifing its prey
And sinking back to its lair
Hidden, it feeds.

*Steven Burt  (10)*
*St Hilary CP School, Truro*

## NIGHT

A black cover creeps over the world at night,
Arriving with moonshine,
Blanking out all but the stars.

Stealthily moving around the world
Giving night,
Black ink that blinds mankind.

Scared by the darkness children shelter under
Comforting bedclothes.

Predatory animals hunt their prey,
Their large eyes
Probe the hidden depths.

As dawn arrives the blanket lifts
Back into the sky like a rocket,
Light returns.

*James Preston (10)*
*St Hilary CP School, Truro*


## THE KANGAROO

The kangaroo is a bouncy ball
Springing across the driest land
Its fur as coarse as an old football
Eyes as dark as the ball's patterned diamonds.

With legs like giant recoiling springs
It bounds across the ground
With no worries at all
Just like a pelted ball.

*Stephanie Jilbert (10)*
*St Hilary CP School, Truro*

## THE WIND

Howling in the night
The beast prowls the dark street
Rattling the windows
Clawing at the roof tiles
And tearing up boxes with his teeth.

He roars like an earthquake
While the fog of his breath
Washes over his prey
As he grabs and eats all he sees.

There is no escape from
His all-consuming mouth
Until satisfied
The beast moves on
Searching
Always searching.

*Tom Robbens (11)*
*St Hilary CP School, Truro*


## THE SHARK AND THE DART

The shark darts across the water
Gliding as if it was heading for a triple twenty,
His teeth as sharp as a dart on the prowl,
Blinding you as it shoots past.

Darting in and out of things in the way,
Hunting around for the bull's-eye
He suddenly finds what he is looking for.
He is ready to attack
And dives straight for the heart.

*Terry Bryant (11)*
*St Hilary CP School, Truro*

## THE STORM

A giant fan within the sky
Creates, at first, a gentle breeze
Then winds itself into a ferocious gale.
Huge waves march like soldiers,
Rank upon rank invade the harbour
Smashing boats into matchsticks.
Roof after roof is tugged at its corners
As the storm inspects each house
And tiles fly like deadly frisbees.
Streets lie littered like a battleground
In the calm after the storm.

*Samuel Clemo  (11)*
*St Hilary CP School, Truro*


## SHARK

Fast blowing tornado,
Tall twisting funnel,
Spinning round and round,
Looking for its prey.
Glistening sharp white teeth
Swaying and swirling
Huge monstrous beast,
Blowing and destroying.
Devouring anything in its path
Then slows down,
Leaving a mountain of destruction.

*Michael Cross  (10)*
*St Hilary CP School, Truro*

## THE FISH

Smooth and shiny as a flowing river
Feel it tickle your fingers
As it speeds on its way
Growing bigger like its harbour.

See it dart swiftly between rocks
Shining and glistening in the morning sunlight
Like reflections from a newly cleaned mirror.

See it leap high in the air like a cannon shell
Then land with a splash
In the deep blue water.

Its destination the sea
Where free from travels
The fish prances, displays
And shoals.

*Megan Westley  (10)*
*St Hilary CP School, Truro*


## THE SEA

The sea a huge monster
Roaring like thunder
Baring sharp white teeth
Pounding up the beach
He demolishes all in his path
Without mercy, grabbing seaweed
And sandhoppers
He retreats to his watery lair
Devours the victims
And finally sleeps.

*Jeremy Mepham  (10)*
*St Hilary CP School, Truro*

## THE WIND

The wind is a wailing wolf
He is a brutal killer
Who leaves a trail of destruction
Wherever he goes.
He throws up the dust
Into his powerful body
And then shakes it off
Miles away.
He is a vacuum cleaner
Who sucks up trees
And then spits out the remains
With the cruel taste.

There is fire in his heart
And he ruthlessly pounces on
All things that lie in his path.
He marks his territory
With broken branches,
Damaged hedgerows
And tumbled iron gates.

He is stealthy and holds no mercy
He builds up his pace as he goes
But soon he will become tired
Because after a while in this massive rage,
His energy becomes faint with
His blows.
Soon he is a docile dog
No longer a rapacious killer
Now he lies within his domain
So still there is barely a shimmer.

*Simon Nellist (11)*
*St Hilary CP School, Truro*

## LION

A lion's mane is a shabby rug,
Tugged and pulled by the night-time breezes,
A soft teddy bear
Wrapped around its neck.

Crawling and prowling
Around its prey
Playing a game
Like a cat with a mouse.

Pouncing high like a gymnast
From a springboard
The lion squeezes the breath from
Its unfortunate victim.

With a loud roar, deep
As a bass drum,
His family are summoned
To the feast he provided.

*Jeremy Kent  (11)*
*St Hilary CP School, Truro*


## AARON

Aaron is a red danger zone.
He is a crazy wasp who has lost his queen.
He is in a playground stinging everyone.
He is a storm out at sea taking his feelings out on a boat.
His clothing is ragged just like his feelings and emotions.
He is a hard table because he cannot open up.
He is like a thriller, you never know what will happen next.
He is a cold, smooth dish of semolina.

*Laura Cocking  (10)*
*St Ives Junior School*

## ALIEN INVASION

Far away in outer space
Aliens are planning to invade our human race
Disguised as helpless rabbits
They arrive on planet earth
Complete with razor-sharp teeth
That really, really hurt
Not a minute had they been here
They set their hair-brained plan in motion
Jumped in the River Thames
Swam way out to the ocean
The mother ship sent down a bomb
That could blow the world sky-high
Then they entered London
Paid a visit to the Queen
(Remember this is part of their hair-brained scheme)
They stole her most prized corgi
And took it far away
This made the whole world really mad
And the Queen ever, ever so sad
The army had no chance against the alien technology
And just when it seemed that we had lost
The Enterprise appeared
They blasted all the aliens
And saved the corgi too
The Queen awarded medals to the Enterprise's crew
And now our world is safe
Oh no, not quite because
One rabbit stayed at base
And is now wandering on earth!

*Amelia Sutherland  (10)*
*St Ives Junior School*

# THE JUNGLE

The beavers gnaw,
The jaguars roar,
In the living jungle.

The macaws chirp,
The monkeys burp,
In the lively jungle.

Far away,
The otters play,
In the wild jungle.

In the distance the orang-utans call,
As a great big elm tree falls,
In the noisy jungle.

Trees knocked down one by one,
Two woodcutters come chopping down some,
In the dying jungle.

As the jungles are disappearing,
People can't help passing and hearing,
Where there was a jungle.

Soon the jungles will all be gone,
Save the jungles one by one.

*Dean Bungay  (10)*
*St Ives Junior School*

## THE OZONE LAYER'S POINT OF VIEW

'Oh these stupid aerosol cans,
dumped fridges
and foam packaging,
they are ruining me
by making holes.
All the time
I am just lying here
stretched around the earth
to protect those things called humans.
I'm always staring at the stars
and other planets.
The sun is really annoying,
it shines right in my eyes
and burns me.
If only those humans were up here
they would know what it's like.'

*James Moon  (10)*
*St Ives Junior School*

## ACID RAIN

A  cid rain is really bad,
C  ause there's things like car exhausts that make it glad.
I  ncredibly the plants die as well,
D  on't worry though we can help.

R  ainforests will die if we don't act quickly,
A  nd we've got a lot of dead trees,
I  nstantly we might get no acid rain,
N  ow let's cross our fingers and hope for the best.

*Jamie Bryce  (10)*
*St Ives Junior School*

## INSIDE AND OUTSIDE

Inside it's like a hot sauna,
Outside the wind howling like a roaring lion.
Inside I feel safe and secure,
Outside I would feel cold and stiff.
Inside I can eat hot food,
Outside I would have to wait.
Inside I am nice and dry,
Outside it is wet.
Inside the fire is roaring,
Outside the wind is howling.
Inside there is no rain just dryness,
Outside it is pouring down with rain.
Inside it is nice and colourful,
Outside it is boring, dull,
At the moment inside is my favourite place.

*Jacqueline Luckham  (9)*
*St Ives Junior School*


## GLOBAL WARMING

You can imagine global warming as a greenhouse.
The heat comes in and it can't get out.
I hear a shout 'Oh no, a drought!'
Make hose-pipe bans, just do what we can,
just turn on the fans, recycle your cans.
What is the solution to pollution?
Think of ideas and make your contribution.
It's up to you, but it's a shame that so few can
even be bothered.
So get up and go because the earth doesn't think
you're a friend, it thinks you're a foe.

*Nicholas Quarton-Cats  (10)*
*St Ives Junior School*

## BORING BORING SCHOOL SCHOOL SCHOOL

Boring boring school school school.
I hate school dinners and homework too.
There's science, geography and history
and handwriting which I have to do again and again
and again.

Boring boring school school school.
I have to stay behind to write my work out once more.
Why do they have to make school such a total bore?

Boring boring school school school.
Discos are a rip off,
Yucky dinners in the hall.

Wicked wicked school school school.
Drawing, chess and draughts,
Races and football.

*Christopher Lock  (10)*
*St Ives Junior School*


## THE OCEAN IS A SEA MONSTER

The ocean is a raging sea monster,
Rushing through the sea.
When he reaches the beach end,
He pounces up at me.

The ocean is a wild sea monster,
Riding on the waves.
Crashing, bashing, rumbling and gnashing,
Are all the noises he makes.

The ocean is a crazy sea monster,
Clashing on the stones.
Dragging them into his lair, the sea,
Like old, human bones.

The ocean is a cruel sea monster,
Picking on anything that dares.
Anything or anyone,
He just doesn't really care . . .

*Charlotte Johnson (11)*
*St Ives Junior School*

## MR GLEESON

He's big and tall,
He rules the school,
Grey hair, hazel eyes,
And he always wears coloured ties,
He works in our class,
He goes red when somebody gets on his nerves,
He always roams the school,
He always says 'Thank you for putting your hand up,'
He's a giggler,
Very polite,
A kind of moaner,
Very serious with practical things,
He always does maths and is very good at spoiling us,
If you ask him one question, he explains the rest of the sheet to you,
He's lost most of his hair,
Because we drive him round the bend.

*Luke Tierney (10)*
*St Ives Junior School*

## GREENHOUSE GASES

Greenhouse gases no, no, no
Carbon dioxide, methane
Nitrous oxide, CFCs
Destroy the world, with great ease.

Cows, cars, fridges and aerosols
Kill the ozone above the world
Heating the world like a greenhouse
Killing all life forms very fast.

But humans can prevent it from happening
By thinking together and co-operating
We can stop the greenhouse effect
And stop the world from being a reject.

*Thomas Emery (11)*
*St Ives Junior School*


## ALIENS!

A  liens, aliens landed on the lawn,
L  anded in the back garden,
I  'm hiding under the covers,
E  specially as they are creeping up the stairs,
N  ow they are in my room, aaarrhh!
S  taring into my eyes.

'A  liens,' I screamed and sat up in bed,
'L  anded in the back garden,' I screamed again,
'I  nto bed, there's no aliens,' said mum,
E  ygh! A sigh of relief, just a dream, no aliens,
N  estling into bed, I look out of the window,
S  tanding there, an alien, looking into my eyes!

*Izzy Dean (10)*
*St Ives Junior School*

# MAGIC MUSHROOMS

In the night when we're all asleep,
Magic mushrooms start to leap,
They open up their magic pores,
Then let out their magic spores.

In the day they're dull and white,
But in the night they're pink and bright,
They really are a freak of nature,
I'm sure they'd make a funny picture.

In the night when we're all asleep,
Magic mushrooms start to leap,
They leap and sing till the night is done,
Then go to sleep with the morning sun.

*Sylvia Myers  (11)*
*St Mark's CE Primary School, Morwenstow*

# TIGGER

I have a dog called Tigger,
She's sweet and cuddly and a good digger.
Her white shiny coat is usually brown,
With brown sloppy mud at which I frown,
We bath her and bath her but it's a waste of time,
Because she'll just play in the slime,
At night-time she's nice and shiny but by dinner time
The following day
*She's muddy again!*

*Emma Olde  (9)*
*St Mark's CE Primary School, Morwenstow*

# MY BABY MONSTER!

My baby monster is quite a pain,
He flicks me and kicks me and whips me with his cane,
Whenever he hurts me I hurt him back,
Then he starts wailing and mum gives me a smack.

My baby monster he is a twit,
He has a brain truly as thick as a brick,
He giggles and laughs and plays tricks on me,
I get so cross mum sends me to bed without any tea.

My baby monster spoke to me,
He said 'You are a flea,'
I got so angry I cut his knee,
He cried and cried and mum grounded me.

*Laura Johns (11)*
*St Mark's CE Primary School, Morwenstow*


# CUMULUS-NIMBUS

Black angry skies are coming,
Bucking gales, thunderbolts, lightning,
Hurricanes are coming,
Twisters raging hail,
Striking lightning in the night,
Tornadoes, vicious rain on the window-pane stinging your head,
*Gigantic Cumulus-Nimbus has led.*

*Liam Bailey (9)*
*St Mark's CE Primary School, Morwenstow*

## LIGHT

Light is bright
It goes at night.
The sun is hot
It brought up a spot.

At morning
The sun is dawning.
At dusk
The sun is yawning.

Light is nice
It comes in a trice.
I like light
It is so bright.

*Kate Gunning  (10)*
*St Mark's CE Primary School, Morwenstow*


## FIREWORKS NIGHT

Traffic light, burning bright,
Catherine wheel, hot to feel,
Chinese dragon, a flying wagon,
And sparklers break the darkness.

Silver rain, too hot for a drain,
Chinese fountain, sprays up like a mountain
Roman candle, warm to handle,
And sparklers break the darkness.

*Victoria Bramhill  (11)*
*St Mark's CE Primary School, Morwenstow*

# MUD

Squish, squash, squish goes
The mud through my toes
Oozing in and out
And all around about.
'Though it does sound kinda mucky
It's really rather lovely
And that's the reason why I like mud!

*Harry Forrest  (9)*
*St Mark's CE Primary School, Morwenstow*


# SPRING

Spring is snowdrops carrying out their life-cycle
Spring is the graceful skylark keeping a watchful eye over its nest
Spring is the primroses bursting from the ground
Spring is rooks building their nests
Spring is insects of all shapes and sizes
Spring is newts in the pond
Spring is wonderful.

*William Bellairs  (9)*
*St Mark's CE Primary School, Morwenstow*


# THE HAND

This is the hand,
that stroked the dog,
that ran over the field
in the misty fog.
This is the hand
that every day
helps me write, work and play.

*Daniel Smith  (9)*
*St Mark's CE Primary School, Morwenstow*

## SMUDGE

*(To my darling baby Smudge who was run over not long after this poem was written at the age of 5 months)*

Smudge is my kitten
loads of fun.
Smudge is mischievous
sweet as a bun.
Smudge is my friend
forever more.
Smudge is squeakier
than an old door.

Smudge is up early
miaowing at dawn.
Smudge is as sweet
as a new fawn.
Smudge is as smooth
as a fur coat.
Smudge is always purring
in her throat.

Smudge can jump
and Smudge can climb.
Smudge is happy
all the time.
Smudge likes her food
and Smudge likes her drink.
but Smudge does not like
playing in the sink.

***Kimberly Hemming  (9)***
***St Mark's CE Primary School, Morwenstow***

## AGES IN STAGES

When I was one I ate a bun,
When I was two I lost my shoe,
When I was three my mum lost me,
When I was four I banged a door,
When I was five I fell on a hive,
When I was six I licked a stick,
When I was seven I went to Devon,
When I was eight I saw my mate,
When I was nine I saw a mine,
   .   That is the age I am.

*Teresa Hobbs  (10)*
*St Mark's CE Primary School, Morwenstow*


## SPRINGTIME

Spring is swollen buds, ready to burst.
Primroses are bursting from their buds.
Rooks building their nests.
It's time for lambs to be born.
Newts swimming to the surface
Gulping for air.

The sun is coming out,
It's getting warmer already. There are
Many newts in the pond.
Easter is coming soon.

*James Allen  (9)*
*St Mark's CE Primary School, Morwenstow*

## SPRING

Skylarks are singing songs in the sky
Primroses are bursting out of their buds
Rabbits are playing in the fields
I played outside with my friends
No going back to winter now
Green grass is growing.

The time is spring,
Inside I hear
My mum is making
Easter eggs.

*Madeleine Powell (8)*
*St Mark's CE Primary School, Morwenstow*

## SPRING

Spring is
Puppies pouncing in the gardens
Rushing rivers in the woods
Nights are getting lighter
Green grass is growing
Tadpoles swimming in the pond
Insects visiting the spring flowers
Morning light
Easter's on its way.

*Lucy Cholwill (9)*
*St Mark's CE Primary School, Morwenstow*

## SPRING IS

Spring is daffodils dancing,
Animals being born,
Rooks building their nests,
Days are getting warmer,
Evenings are getting lighter,
Skylarks singing in the sky guarding their nests,
Spring is lichen hanging from the apple trees in the
nature reserve.
Spring is swollen buds ready to burst,
Spring is rabbits grazing on the fresh green grass.
        Spring is . . .

*Caroline Hobbs  (9)*
*St Mark's CE Primary School, Morwenstow*

## SPRING

Spring is snowdrops swaying in the breeze,
Spring is daffodils dancing,
Spring is primroses peeping up through the brambles,
Spring is lambs leaping,
Spring is birds singing to mark their territory,
Spring is birds singing to attract a mate,
Spring is newts coming up to the surface
And breathing.
*Spring is wonderful.*

*Emily Pool  (8)*
*St Mark's CE Primary School, Morwenstow*

## SPRING

Spring is
Primroses ready to burst open
Rabbits chewing on the fresh green grass
In the sun
Night-times are getting warmer
Geese are having their little goslings

Tadpoles swimming
In the ponds
Moles digging in the garden
Easter on its way.

*Andrew Hobbs  (9)*
*St Mark's CE Primary School, Morwenstow*

## MY KITTEN

Black as night,
An amber streak,
Down her nose,
One amber paw.

Lovely and cuddly,
Like a teddy bear,
All warm and snuggly,
Cosy as a jumper.

Purring like an engine,
Or miaowing for her food,
Scratching at the door,
'Let me in'.

*Laura Jane Goddard  (8)*
*St Martin's J&I School, Isles of Scilly*

## THE SEA

Smooth glassy water,
Calm and gentle,
Sparkling like a diamond,
Catching a rainbow.

Fierce and dangerous,
When the storm comes,
Crashing against rocks,
Spray splashing,
White water curving as it drops.

*Charlotte Mary Jane (9)*
*St Martin's J&I School, Isles of Scilly*


## THE BLOODTHIRSTY LION

The pounding wind lashing
the people with fear.
The fear of bloodthirsty fangs.
With flashing fists,
blasting the gates of houses.
At the same time spitting bolts of
lightning,
so blinding that you can't see.
The roaring wind so powerful that it
could deafen you,
it's like stamping feet of a lion,
prancing at its food.
But it is still thirsty, thirsty for more.
So it hunts and hunts until it has
done its work.

*Cain Herlihy (10)*
*St Mary's RC School, Falmouth*

## PHANTOM HUMAN BEING

I have seen and heard of many scary things,
But worst of all,
The most fearsome thing to me,
Is a phantom human being.
They say it's all in your mind,
They say it's your brain working
Overtime,
But that's very hard to believe,
When everyone's asleep and,
They're larking around your room,
Keeping you awake,
Leaping, jumping,
Prowling, scrowling.
But they're not
Sad,
Oh no, in fact they find great pleasure in
Scaring us out of our wits.
It's morning,
It's over,
Once again they're hiding.
But they'll be back,
I know.

*David Robinson (11)*
*St Mary's RC School, Falmouth*

# THINGS THAT FLY

Things that fly,
Make me realise why.
Why can't we fly?
Do we have to apply?
It would be great,
But there would probably be a debate.
We would have wings,
Just like we have kings.
People might get scared,
Clothes will get teared.
When people try to fly from a tree,
They make all the birds flee innocently.
There's my poem about things that fly,
Now make sure that you don't try.

*Russell Amos (11)*
*St Mary's RC School, Falmouth*


## MAKING BISCUITS

Cooking, cooking
is such
*fun*
especially when you get to
*eat*
the buns.
You weigh the things
and get it right
and smell the delicious buns.
You sieve the sugar
like the snow
and wait until
it is done.

*Sadye McAulay (9)*
*St Mellion VA CE School, Saltash*

## SHINING SUN

The sun
shines on me
and makes me
happy
and jumpy.

The spring sun
shines on
the flowers
and makes them
come alive.

The golden sun
shines on
the grass
and makes daisies
and buttercups
pop out.

The glaring sun
shines on
the flowers
and grass
and we can
*play.*

***Richard Abraham  (7)***
***St Mellion VA CE School, Saltash***

## SPRING

The daffodil
gazes in the daylight
It sways in the sun
the refreshing wind
refreshes it
The flower glows
and awakes
it is rising from the dead
The puffing sound of the wind
as spring battles winter
Spring has won
but winter still pushes
day by day
as our shadows
stick to us
We get annoyed
so we run.

*Charles Henning  (8)*
*St Mellion VA CE School, Saltash*


## SPRING FUN

The golden shine of the sun
Lets us have lots of fun
The peeping flowers
Up they come
To have a little fun
Then they grow
For some sun
Until they find it
Lots of fun.

*Robert Pridham  (7)*
*St Mellion VA CE School, Saltash*

## SNOWMAN

I am as cold
as anything.
People shove
sticks
in my body.
They put a
carrot
in my head.
They put
pebbles
on my head.
They put a
hat
on my head
and pebbles
near the hat.
They make me
look like a person.

*Daniel Lee  (7)*
*St Mellion VA CE School, Saltash*


## SPRING TO SUMMER

The golden sun is shining in the school playground.
Children playing with their shadows, chasing them all ways.
Playing games makes us feel happy.
Calm winds in the fresh springtime.
Daffodils waking up, popping out of the soil.
Primroses pushing out.
The sun dazzles my eyes and the shining glow of the sun
gently comes into the summer sun.

*James Bock  (8)*
*St Mellion VA CE School, Saltash*

## SPRING

My shadow follows me
wherever I go
whatever I do
whatever I see
whatever I hear
he's always there next to me.

The buds are blossoming
the trees are awakening
the animals come out from hibernating.
The winter's biting wind
has been taken over
by the spring's gentle breeze.

Where are the
winter clouds?
Winter is gone.
Here come the birds
here comes the cheer.

*Joseph Henning (10)*
*St Mellion VA CE School, Saltash*

## THE SUN

Shining sun on top of you
Shining golden down at us
A sun glowing at you
Shining sun on you
It makes shadows under you
It shines in your eyes.

*Cassie Batten (8)*
*St Mellion VA CE School, Saltash*

## THE STORY OF THE SUN

Morning comes and
the sun awakes.
It gives a golden shine.
It starts to rise
into the sky.
Then it starts to dazzle.
People wake up.
They see the light
of the sun
and feel the
nice heat.

It's soon noon.
Everyone's playing
in the hot sun.
People don't dare
to look at the sun
because it will
damage their eyes.

The night comes
the sun doesn't
shine very much.
The sun goes
down in slow motion.
People say goodnight
and wait for the
golden sun
to appear
in the morning.

*Sophie Mace  (9)*
*St Mellion VA CE School, Saltash*

## SPRING

One day I went to play
out in the sunlight's spray
The sun's bright light
on me and the sight
I think it must be spring.

Spring's the king of winter
Winter's like a splinter
prickling your finger
Oh I'm glad it's spring.

The sun splits up into tiny
shreds of gold
The clouds push in
it's time for bed
Let's wait to see the sun
Another spring day.

*Coral McAulay  (11)*
*St Mellion VA CE School, Saltash*


## LIGHT OF SPRING

Winter frosts have dried away
Spring is coming day by day
Daffodils grow strong and bright
Getting warmer through the night.

Animals wake up from their sleep
They go outside to have a peep
Light is shining everywhere
Trees are green, no longer bare.

Children dance, have lots of races
See the smiles on their faces
Birds sing, bees hum
Goodbye winter, spring has come.

**Grant Mace  (10)**
**St Mellion VA CE School, Saltash**

## CHRISTMAS

I am decorated with tinsel
and I stand
*proud*
in a warm house.

I've got
*presents*
under me
with red and green paper.

If you put
*candles*
on me
I can be dangerous.

If you
*decorate*
me properly
I can be
*beautiful.*

What am I?

**Chris Smith  (11)**
**St Mellion VA CE School, Saltash**

## A STREET IN SPRING

In the spring as I come to a street,
I can see people eating wheat,
Daffodils grow as I look at my feet,
I can feel a special treat.

Come on and follow me,
Come on and follow me.

Looking above at the sky,
It feels like I'm up so high,
Like a bird in the blue sky.

Come on and follow me,
Come on and follow me.

In the spring as I come to the end of a street,
The sun is glaring hot,
People shouting and running about,
Walking still towards the sun,
All the flowers must weigh a tonne.

*Kelly Moore (11)*
*St Mellion VA CE School, Saltash*


## SPRING SHADOWS

Sticky shadows linger
behind you, there's no
escape from your shadow.

I dance, it dances
I run, it follows
it won't go away.
My shadow and I are
now best friends
but my shadow never talks.

The sun goes down
the moon comes up
my shadow disappeared.
I try to dance like before
but still no shadow appears
so I return home for the night
sadly with tears.

*Andrew Smith  (8)*
*St Mellion VA CE School, Saltash*


## THE SUN

The golden sun
shining
on the cottages
Your shadows
are on
your body
they stick on you.
The flowers
are rising
popping up.
The wind
is blowing
flowers away.
Your sticky shadows
are long.
Spring is new
playful and jolly
and fun.
The sun
is glowing
in your face.

*Lee Rice  (8)*
*St Mellion VA CE School, Saltash*

# CHRISTMAS DAY

One fairy had a cherry
on a fine Christmas day.
She had a card
from Uncle Lard
and opened it
on a hard rock.
She had a jelly
that went to her belly
and her name is Kelly.
Kelly got a tree
that was down to her knee
and it was three.
She baked her cake
near a lake
and she scooped
a bit on her plate.
She got a toy
and was full of joy.
One boy was bold
and his head was cold.
The day went
Christmas had gone.

*Jack Batten  (10)*
*St Mellion VA CE School, Saltash*

## COOKING

The smells of cooking
come up your nose.
Crumble, buns, cakes
and coconuts.
Buns smell delicious,
sugar is sweet.
I would like to eat sugar.
Sugar mixed up with butter
gives me a flutter,
not forgetting the butter.
Flour is from a flower.
Flowers grow outside
but flour is something you
mix up in a bowl.

*Jason Edwards (9)*
*St Mellion VA CE School, Saltash*


## THE FUN OF COOKING

Cooking is fun,
when you can eat a luscious bun,
chocolate chip
and cherry bits,
grams, grams
and strawberry jams,
tickling taste buds
are better than soap suds,
sugar that's sweet
what a treat.

*Thomas Lee (10)*
*St Mellion VA CE School, Saltash*

## COOKING BISCUITS

Today we did cooking
it was very fun.
The butter was squidgy
the flour was soft.
We were making biscuits
but we had to weigh
the ingredients.
We could have anything
in the biscuits,
but I had to have
gorgeous
chocolate chips.
I couldn't wait
to eat it all up.

*Ross Painter (10)*
*St Mellion VA CE School, Saltash*


## BISCUITS AND BUNS

Cooking is fun,
Making biscuits and buns,
Chocolate chip and cherry,
Melting butter in your hands,
Cutting different shapes,
Stars, dogs, trees and hearts,
Weighing sugar and flour,
Can't wait to put them in the oven,
But wait until you try one,
Mouth-watering,
Mmmm . . .
           *Delicious.*

*Holly Baker (9)*
*St Mellion VA CE School, Saltash*

## MY TWO FRIENDS

My two friends are really funny,
we have fun and muck about.
They are both different people,
we talk until the end of play.
We go to each other's houses,
one is funny and one is weird.
One is tall and one is small.
One of them has short brown hair and
one of them has short blonde hair.
They are very sporty, one plays football
and one plays netball.
We are best friends and will be for a very,
very long time.
Their names are Anna and Sharon.

*Aimee Lourens  (11)*
*St Nicolas VA CE School, Torpoint*


## BISCUITS

Oh look all the biscuits have gone
They have not been there very long
Little girls and little boys
Took them out with oh so little noise
Boys like ginger ones
Girls like orange buns
But looking through the kitchen door
Great, mum's already making more.

*Vivienne Pengelly  (10)*
*St Nicolas VA CE School, Torpoint*

## FOOTBALL - LIVERPOOL VS MANCHESTER

Toss a coin in the air,
it goes round and round,
before it hits the ground.
Heads or tails, heads it is.
The Pool has won the toss,
we'll show you who's boss.
There goes the whistle.
A pass, a dribble, a chance to change the score.
Oh no, nice save, Man U keep it nil-nil.
A kick by Smick, a boot by Cole.
A save by James, a pass, a dribble, a goal.
The crowd goes wild.
The final whistle.
Liverpool one, Man U nil.

*Ben Booth  (9)*
*St Nicolas VA CE School, Torpoint*

## THE ENVIRONMENT

The environment comes in loads of different ways,
If you don't use it correctly you will pay.
So don't you forget the environment needs
loads of different creatures just like these:
The laughing hyena,
The jumping kangaroo,
The very slimy snake,
Who might eat you.

*Suzzi Porter  (10)*
*St Nicolas VA CE School, Torpoint*

## WONDER WHAT THE WHITENESS IS
*(To Tosca, with love)*

She stares out of the window,
Wondering what it is.
She talks to it,
It does not answer.
She goes out.
Ouch, what is it?
She licks it off her little black nose.
More comes, it's cold.
It's a beautiful creamy-white.
It comes down as quietly as torn tissue paper.
Floating, flying, drifting, touching and resting.
She goes inside.
People are communicating in strange noises.
'How are we going to get the car out, the snow's
blocked the road?'
She goes to sleep, her head resting on someone's leg.

*Elinor Huggett  (9)*
*St Nicolas VA CE School, Torpoint*

## MY CAT RUSTY

My cat Rusty is as swift as a leopard.
My cat Rusty is like a rusty old car.
My cat Rusty is as sweet as a dormouse.
She even gives you her paw.
My cat Rusty puts up a fight.
My cat Rusty is always on top.
My cat Rusty chases little birds.
My cat Rusty is the sweetest cat alive.

*Chloe Hubbard  (10)*
*St Nicolas VA CE School, Torpoint*

## GOALIES

Goalies must be hard.
Goalies must be tough.
Goalies need to eat lots of stuff,
Because goalies must be rough.
Dive for the ball, you've got to be quick,
If not consequences could make you sick.
The ball is coming up, it's going in the net.
No way! *I'm* in goal.
A player has been knocked down,
It's going to be a free kick.
Oh no! I feel sick.
The game is over, I'm going home.

*Dean Tiltman (11)*
*St Nicolas VA CE School, Torpoint*


## FRIENDS

Friends can be small,
Friends can be big,
Some can be poor,
Some can be rich,
They can be black and white,
They can be fat and thin,
Friends can be boring and fun,
They come from all around the world,
Friends are kind and buy you things,

Best of all is to have a friend that you like.

*Anna Luff (10)*
*St Nicolas VA CE School, Torpoint*

## WHAT ARE FRIENDS FOR?

Friends are tall and thin
Friends are short and stout
Friends are always there for you
You never will fall out
Friends are friends through day and night
Through good and bad
Every step in life you take, there's a friend
Around every bend
My friends' names are David, Sue, Tom and Lue.

*Amy Gladdish  (9)*
*St Nicolas VA CE School, Torpoint*

## A PIRATE FROM POD

There was a pirate from Pod
Who had a fishing rod.
He went for a float,
In his boat.
He came into Pod
Carrying a cod.
The people cheered,
Waving their beards
And the pirate was famous in Pod.

*Jake Gladdish  (11)*
*St Nicolas VA CE School, Torpoint*

## MY STREET

On my street
It is very strange
There's a cat with a tail
Curled up like a snail
It is black and hairy
And runs around
It makes this awful screeching sound
It keeps me awake all night long
And all of a sudden I hear a great big *bong!*

The bong I hear is a mere tear
Of the giant who lives next door
He cries with a tear
As big as a can of beer
Just as I start to get to sleep
I hear a very high-pitched *squeak!*

The squeak is a cry of an owl calling
In fact as I speak he seems to be falling
He falls to the ground with a great big thump
Or is that the sound of the antelope?

The antelope stampede by
'Oh no' as I start to sigh
He goes past my window and
I look up in the sky
As I look Mr and Mrs Dracula fly by.

We're very good friends with them you know
Well look at me I am as white as snow
Oh look, here I go
Up in the sky and past the post
Well actually I am a *ghost!*

*Hannah Howarth  (10)*
*St Nicolas VA CE School, Torpoint*

## THE THUNDERSTORM

The rain began to fall,
Slamming against the window-pane,
Like little impy footsteps,
I was scared.

The puffy white clouds,
Went scuttling away,
And dark ones took their place,
I was scared.

The clouds began to growl,
Like big bad dogs,
Then lightning crashed!
I was scared.

A yellow streak across the sky,
The big black clouds in the night,
Rain falling on the window,
I was scared.

Then I fell asleep,
And when I woke up,
It was all gone,
I wasn't scared any more.

*Charlotte Cade  (10)*
*St Nicolas VA CE School, Torpoint*

## MY HAMSTER, APRICOT CHERRY

At night my hamster
scuttles in his wheel.
'Rattle, rattle, rattle'.

He sits and he eats.
'Nibble, nibble, nibble'.

My hamster drinks fast.
'Slurp, slurp, slurp'.

My hamster smells his new clean cage.
'Sniff, sniff, sniff'.

My hamster talks.
'Squeak, squeak, squeak.'

My hamster's delicate nose moves.
'Twitch, twitch, twitch'.

This is all about my hamster
Apricot Cherry.

*Sharon Broad  (11)*
*St Nicolas VA CE School, Torpoint*


## YELLOW BELLOWS

Hi, my name is Bellow
and I'm a jolly good fellow
I always wear yellow
because I'm a jolly good fellow
So I have to wear yellow
because Bellows wear yellows.

*Tom Fear  (9)*
*St Nicolas VA CE School, Torpoint*

## OUR WORLD

Car fumes,
Factories,
Sewage
And junk,
That's our world.
Pollution,
Gases,
Poison,
And drugs,
That's our world.
Guns,
Wars,
Bombs
And homeless,
That's our world.
Vandalism,
Racism,
Mugs
And bullies,
That's our world,
Let's change it.

*Josie Elston (10)*
*St Nicolas VA CE School, Torpoint*


## RED

As a fire glows
A devil stands there eating juicy apples.
Lipstick sparkling on the devil's lips.
Wine running down my throat.
Blood is coming out of me.
A cauldron standing with potions mixing around.

*Stacey Lobb (9)*
*St Paul's CP Junior School, Penzance*

## WINTER

A white blanket stretches across the knobbly land,
Frozen ponds that no longer ripple,
Bare and lonely trees stand with no life,
An endless flood of rain falls from the never ending sky,
A sign of life seems to retire,
Seas are forming into a roaring wave,
That becomes the sailor's grave.

*Anne-Marie Bolitho  (9)*
*St Paul's CP Junior School, Penzance*


## A RECIPE FOR SPRING

Mix a cupful of flowers into a bowlful of blossom.
Add a tablespoon of sunshine.
Whisk a jugful of rain into a bowlful of daffodils.
Stir in a handful of fresh air.
Cook in the oven for an hour.
Serve with a dusting of buds.

*Kirstin Sibley  (7)*
*St Paul's CP Junior School, Penzance*


## A RECIPE FOR SPRING

Mix a bowlful of buds.
Sprinkle a teaspoon of grass.
Add a handful of daffodils
With a jugful of fresh air.
Then put in a tablespoon of rain.
Bake in oven for an hour.
Then serve with a sprinkling of blossom.

*Kirsten Perry  (7)*
*St Paul's CP Junior School, Penzance*

## MUM

A nappy-changer
A house-cleaner
A dinner-cooker
A table-layer
A hard-worker
A hair-plaiter
A bed-maker
A washing-hanger
A guinea pig-minder
A dog-walker
A quick gardener
A homework-helper
A silent reader
A TV-watcher.

*Sally Payne (10)*
*St Paul's CP Junior School, Penzance*


## A MONKEY

A banana-eater
A big muncher
A tree-swinger
An insect-catcher
A food-stealer
A big jumper
A tree-dangler
A nut-lover
A warm snuggler
A night sleeper.

*Stacey Blackmore (10)*
*St Paul's CP Junior School, Penzance*

## WINTER

A blanket of white
covering the land.
The grass is still.
A man called Jack Frost
has painted it in a coat of
pure white.
A big puddle of frozen
water is a dent in the
pavement.
It looks like a skating rink.
The trees plain, with icicles hanging
from the branches.
They swing around in the
mad wind.
Fences crack and fall to the ground.
People try hard to walk and the
wind tries to stop them.

*Ben Bodilly  (10)*
*St Paul's CP Junior School, Penzance*


## GREY

A foggy hilltop,
With scattered graveyards.
Scary skeletons come back from the dead,
Unknown spirits and ghosts,
A dull winter's day.
Fish swim in the dark lonely sea,
Electric eels light up the fishes' way.

*David Brookes  (9)*
*St Paul's CP Junior School, Penzance*

## MY SIMILE ABOUT SALLY PAYNE

Sally is as friendly as a rabbit
Sally's face is as white as snow
Sally's eyes are as brown as chocolate buttons
Sally's cheeks are as red as blood
Sally's eyelashes are as long as a piece of cotton
Sally's skin is as smooth as silk.

*Amy Richards  (10)*
*St Paul's CP Junior School, Penzance*


## I'D RATHER BE

I'd rather be a dog than a cat.
I'd rather be thin than fat.
I'd rather be a ball than a bat.
I'd rather be stood than sat.
I'd rather be a fly than a gnat.
I'd rather be a mouse than a rat.

*Hannah Jeckells  (9)*
*St Paul's CP Junior School, Penzance*


## I'D RATHER BE

I'd rather be thin than fat
I'd rather be a rag than a bag
I'd rather be a rug than a mat
I'd rather be a dog than a cat
I'd rather be bumpy than flat
I'd rather be a bird than a bat
I'd rather be a fly than a gnat.

*Aaron Fawley  (9)*
*St Paul's CP Junior School, Penzance*

# I SAW A . . .

I saw a dolphin eat a rat.
I saw a cat hit a bat.
I saw a rat branching out.
I saw a tree practising for ballet.
I saw a girl jump a bog.
I saw a boy being put in the wash.
I saw a sock drink cider.
I saw a spider being hit with a mat.
I saw a rat put on his belt.
I saw my dad blow his nose.
I saw Mr De-seta sniff a rose.
I saw Mrs Ash melt in the sun.
I saw a snowman being swallowed.
I saw a swallow being picked.
I saw a flower flip and flap.

*Rebecca Andrews (9)*
*St Paul's CP Junior School, Penzance*


# A WINTER'S DREAM

Today it is raining and cold too
But here I lie in my warm bed
I don't mind if it rains in the night
While I'm asleep dreaming my winter's dream
I dream of animals warm and dry
Cosy cottages with warm wood fires
But my winter's dream is cold
Cold enough for gale force winds and hail
Making a noise against the window
Like a beggar knocking on the door in the rain
Because a winter's dream is a dream.

*Jessica Davy-Thomas (9)*
*St Paul's CP Junior School, Penzance*

## I'D RATHER BE . . .

I'd rather be a blue carpet than a mat.
I'd rather be a grey mouse than a cat.
I'd rather be stood than sat.
I'd rather be on concrete than on a lap.
I'd rather be a bee than a tap.
I'd rather be a bird than a hat.
I'd rather be thin than fat.
I'd rather be filled than have a gap.
I'd rather be a shark than a bat.
I'd rather be a person than a map.
I'd rather be square than flat.
I'd rather be a big bear than a rat.

*Sasha Carter  (10)*
*St Paul's CP Junior School, Penzance*


## HAIKU POEM

Snow is a blanket
Like a layer of feathers
But frost takes over.

Hail falling straight down
A downpour is very hard
As soon as it lands.

Strikes at the speed of sound
With bad burns to a city
Skyscrapers toppling.

*Eve Parker  (10)*
*St Paul's CP Junior School, Penzance*

# TOM

A mucky eater
A bottle-feeder
A thumb-sucker
A hair-puller
A dummy-sucker
A good crier
A bad sleeper
A milk-eater
A gurgle-maker
A cuddle-bringer
A rice-eater
A puddle-bringer.

*Laura McGarry (9)*
*St Paul's CP Junior School, Penzance*

# I SAW A POEM

I saw jelly swaying around.
I saw a tree walking to school.
I saw a boy eating a nut.
I saw a bird going too fast around town.
I saw the policeman eat some jelly.
I saw a girl as drunk as a skunk.
I saw a man feeding the birds.
I saw a monkey melt in the sun.
I saw my dad doing the boogie.
I saw an ice-cream with a ball around.

*William Trembath (10)*
*St Paul's CP Junior School, Penzance*

## AUTUMN

Fluttering leaves coming down and down
Blocking the drains from town to town
Hedgehogs hibernating, birds flying away
It is time for autumn
Red and brown leaves are falling to the ground
As people walk by they crackle and crunch
Rabbits are making a warm home, oh!
Winter is coming with sparkling white snow.

*Simon Ireland  (10)*
*St Paul's CP Junior School, Penzance*


## WINTER

Plain and bare trees standing
in a chilly, lonely park.
Wet and unpleasant weather
and ponds that have frozen over.
Crunchy, icy and slippery grass
not moving one bit.
Somebody has laid a giant white
sheet everywhere.

*Joel Day  (10)*
*St Paul's CP Junior School, Penzance*


## THE SIMPSONS

Bart's got spiky hair.
Lisa plays the saxophone.
Homer is very fat.
Marge has big bushy blue hair.
Maggie sucks a big dummy.

*Kelly Doyle  (10)*
*St Paul's CP Junior School, Penzance*

## I'D RATHER BE . . .

I'd rather be wise than foolish.
I'd rather be sweets than liquorice.
I'd rather be French than Turkish.
I'd rather be kind than selfish.
I'd rather be a shark than a shellfish.
I'd rather be a plate than a dish.

*Matthew Deponeo (10)*
*St Paul's CP Junior School, Penzance*


## WINTER

Windows are painted with icy patterns by
the blowing winds,
Someone has painted the gardens white overnight,
It looks so bare out there, trees stand alone,
No one noticing them,
The rivers have changed into flooding pools of water,
A magic person has sewn a white blanket and
dropped it over the earth,
Winter is here once again.

*Rebecca McGarry (9)*
*St Paul's CP Junior School, Penzance*


## BLUE

Sea swaying from side to side,
Penguins perched on cold icebergs,
Up above the atmosphere,
An aquarium full of tropical coloured fish,
Neptune up in the massive solar system,
A full moon in the evening wilderness.

*Joshua Poynter (10)*
*St Paul's CP Junior School, Penzance*

# RED

A man wants to get his own back
Eager and angry
Always trying to get revenge
While children sit by the blazing fire
The child is embarrassed, says he can't do the speech
Whilst children eat liquorice
Danger lurks around the corner
And people don't know what lurks in the flames of the fire.

*John Chatwin (9)*
*St Paul's CP Junior School, Penzance*


# ME

I have eyes like the sky,
I have hair like silky candy,
My voice is a light melody
and my teeth glow in the night.
I am the colour yellow,
I am like a roller-coaster,
full of excitement and fun.

*Katie Carswell (9)*
*St Paul's CP Junior School, Penzance*


# RED

Danger looms all around the deserted mansion
Two eager lovers dance by candlelight
Anger is the only thought in the tiny mind of the devil
Warm rays of the fire
A dead dog lies in a pool of his own blood
Roses sense love but somehow danger.

*Tom Starnes (9)*
*St Paul's CP Junior School, Penzance*

## HAIKU CHEETAH

Running like the wind
Trying to capture its prey
Pouncing and chewing.

*Scott Swanson  (10)*
*St Paul's CP Junior School, Penzance*


## SPRING

A new world.
Spring dawns like a bird singing in a choir.
Flowers bud like a new world.
New animals jumping through the air.
It is nice when the flowers bud in the spring.
Spring dawns like a mountain of freshness.

*Mark Darby  (10)*
*St Paul's CP Junior School, Penzance*


## I'D RATHER BE . . .

I'd rather be short than tall.
I'd rather be standing up straight than fall.
I'd rather shout than call.
I'd rather be a bed than a stall.
I'd rather be a shop than a mall.
I'd rather stay at home than be in a brawl.
I'd rather be a door than a wall.
I'd rather be a thin bat than a fat ball.

*Rachel Overduin  (10)*
*St Paul's CP Junior School, Penzance*

## JAGUAR XJ220

Fast as a bullet
Engine roaring very loud
Bombs along the road.

*Matthew Colenso  (9)*
*St Paul's CP Junior School, Penzance*


## WAR

War is as frightening as a spider,
It is as scary as a nightmare,
It is like windows cracking,
It makes a sound like lights blowing up,
It is as deafening as a siren.

*Kelly Paul  (9)*
*St Paul's CP Junior School, Penzance*


## DAFFODILS

With their fat yellow trumpets
They make no noise
They sway in the wind
Like dancing fairies
They grow in fields, hedges everywhere
And when you see them you know spring is here
They stand tall and silent and proud as can be
The most beautiful flower in the world to me.

*Sarah Leonard  (11)*
*St Paul's CP Junior School, Penzance*

## WINTER

We dress up warm in our hats and coats
To face the bitter winds.
The storm clouds gather up in the sky
And huge waves crash upon the rocks
While the boats are safely in the harbour.
The birds try to find some food.
The winter winds whistle and whine.
The icicles hang from my window
As I watch the stinging hail.
I start to shiver.
It is very chilly outside.
I am glad to be inside my lovely warm house.

*Charlotte Rose-Terry  (8)*
*St Paul's CP Junior School, Penzance*

## WINTER

There are icy winds outside, it is very stormy
Everything is being blown away
The winter winds are whistling and whining
The hail crashes on my window
Icicles hang from my window
The huge waves crash on the rocks
While the boats are safe in the harbour
I am warm in bed.

*Max Stokes  (9)*
*St Paul's CP Junior School, Penzance*

## ACTION MAN

I have lots of toys
But the one I like the best
Is my Action Man toy
I put him to the test.

I throw him off the bunk beds
And up and down the stairs
I throw him out the window
And watch him flying through the air.

I have lots of toys
But the one I like the best
Is my Action Man toy
He's better than the rest.

*Matthew Lobb  (7)*
*St Paul's CP Junior School, Penzance*

## SPRING

Smells of spring fill the air,
Pretty daffodils grow and bloom,
Rabbits run in the fields and chase each
                            other's tails,
Indoors it is not much fun, I wish I could be
                            in the sun,
Night takes longer to arrive,
Grass is cut and looking neat,
I think I will go and sit on the garden seat.

*Sophie Ruffell  (8)*
*St Paul's CP Junior School, Penzance*

## THE INCREDIBLE DJ

There was a man called BJ,
He was an incredible DJ,
His records were good,
But no one understood.
Why he was in his PJ.

*Martin Bawden  (8)*
*St Paul's CP Junior School, Penzance*


## A NEW DOG

I saw a lovely dog,
I would really like to love.
She's soft like velvet.
Just like a Hush Puppy dog.
A lady says she needs a home
Someone has treated her badly.
So mummy said we'll give her a home,
We will even buy her a new bone.

*Abby Poynter  (7)*
*St Paul's CP Junior School, Penzance*


## SUMMER DAYS

Spring has passed and what is next?
Unicorns dancing and prancing everywhere.
My mind will never forget the lovely summer.
Millions of birds singing in the fields,
Every little ray of sunshine means a lot to me.
Rainy days are coming back - it is autumn.

*Luke Povey  (7)*
*St Paul's CP Junior School, Penzance*

## BONFIRE NIGHT

As I stood there by the fire,
The glow as bright as sunset.
Sparks go by in a flash
Fireworks shimmer in the dark.

As I hold a sparkler in my hand
I see the colours of the rainbow.
It will shine
No matter what I do.

As I dance and sing
I say at last 'It's bonfire time'
I am here
To dance all night.

As the fire burns low
I see the bright lights in the sky,
And leave the fire,
To say goodbye.

*Kirsty Leonard (8)*
*St Paul's CP Junior School, Penzance*


## SPRINGTIME

In springtime the daffodils bloom.
Baby lambs are born.
Birds are hatching little chicks.
Blossoms are budding.
In the evening it is lighter.
Animals are awakening from hibernation.
Days are becoming warmer.
Trees are growing their leaves.
Soon the summer holidays will be here.

*Tiffen Willis (7)*
*St Paul's CP Junior School, Penzance*

## NATURE

In the garden flowers grow,
In the fields farmers sow,
Grasshoppers noisy in the grass,
Spring has come, winter's past.

Hedgehogs with sleepy eyes,
Birds swoop and fill the skies,
Animals awake - spring has come!
Life returns - winter's done.

Blossom floating in the air,
Seeds are sprouting everywhere.
Corn stalks sway in the breeze,
Fishes swimming in the seas.

Warm sunlight fills the day
Moths and butterflies dance and play.
Birds play and sing their song,
Nature's cycle carries on.

*Samantha Potter (7)*
*St Paul's CP Junior School, Penzance*


## DAFFODILS

Golden trumpets, standing tall,
Regal, stately, by the wall.
Radiant yellow, like the sun,
Heavily perfumed, every one.
Dawn's morning glory fills the woods,
Shimmering and shaking their dainty hoods.
Like glorious crowns on tender stalks,
To be greatly admired on country walks.

*John Watson (10)*
*St Paul's CP Junior School, Penzance*

## RED

Danger is a shocking cross
There is a laughing devil up on the hill.
Wine is trickling down my throat like burning blood.
There's an angry wizard flying around.
Lipstick is the writing all over the wall.
A juicy tomato is rolling down the street.
There is a glistening ruby sticking out of the wall.
There is a hint of air freshener floating in the air.
A rotting strawberry is under the fridge.

*Marc Sims  (10)*
*St Paul's CP Junior School, Penzance*


## A NEW WORLD

Spring dawns like a new life to nature
Colourful collages of flowers cover the ground.
The beautiful fragrance of a new perfume fills the air.
The sweet melody of birds singing in the treetops.
The silent winds whistle softly in the trees.

*Andrew Wills  (11)*
*St Paul's CP Junior School, Penzance*


## NIGHT

The night is a glowing tornado of darkness,
A fierce fighting ocean,
As crazy as a ferocious dog,
A swirling whirlpool of stars,
Deeper than the deepest black hole,
A blinding shield from the bright moon.

*Holly Williams  (11)*
*St Paul's CP Junior School, Penzance*

# FAMINE

The weeping children are not heard,
They are like a single tear in a great ocean,
Happiness is nowhere to be found
Life in a never ending desert
Dry, hard soil
Crumbles in your hand,
Skin tightens by the day.
The sadness in their eyes
Is unspeakable.
Can we hear their cries?
Can we feel their pain?
Mothers feel so helpless
Watching their children die
It is so bad
The people are so weak
One piece of bread is a dream.

*Jessie Hands (11)*
*St Paul's CP Junior School, Penzance*


# A NEW WORLD

Spring dawns like a tree of life,
Branching out for a new year,
It is a mountain of freshness,
Dark winter clouds blow away,
Making way for the clear blue sky.

The winter frost breaks down,
To reveal a riot of plant life,
Snowdrops, daffodils, bluebells all appear,
The prettiest of all is the tulip,
Daffodils spread like a golden cloak.

*Ben Oldcorn (10)*
*St Paul's CP Junior School, Penzance*

## THE PHANTOM

The phantom lies beneath the stage,
To him he is barred in a huge locked cage,
He feels the need to avenge,
He feels the power of revenge,
At the beginning of Act Four,
His lonely feeling comes once more,
He knows the life he used to lead,
And the life the people need,
His unknown past forever haunts,
His mind is full of endless taunts,
His past is now a buried remain,
But still he regards it with great pain.

*Gary Eddy  (11)*
*St Paul's CP Junior School, Penzance*


## DAFFODIL

Daffodils stand like soldiers playing their trumpets
They are seated in a hedge watching the world go by.
Their stems are strong spears
Their petals are tissue paper
They stand tall and firm in the breezy wind,
Dazzling star petals protect the proud trumpet
Daffodils are the gifts of joy and happiness.

*Jonathan Pollard  (11)*
*St Paul's CP Junior School, Penzance*

# DAFFODILS

Daffodils yellow as a pot of butter
Ready to explode.
They cover fields
like a golden blanket of light.
Daffodils, the smallest trumpets
I've ever seen.
The stem is a green paintbrush,
colouring the world.
Daffodils are a golden sunset,
Growing like a bud on a tree.

*Matthew Francis (11)*
*St Paul's CP Junior School, Penzance*

# THE NIGHT

The night is a calm kitten
Dreaming quietly,
A smooth blanket,
Covering the world.
A peaceful black horse,
Galloping on the moors.
A whirling sky of darkness,
A silent pond flowing along,
Silky, noiseless tree blowing with the wind.
Fox eyes glowing with the stars.

*Liane Keast (10)*
*St Paul's CP Junior School, Penzance*

## THE NIGHT

The night is a soft blanket
Of never ending darkness,
A calm kitten,
An owl hooting,
A dog barking,
The moon disappears,
Clouds like a galloping horse,
It is dark out there,
Stars like a meadow of flowers twinkle in the moonlight,
How many hours before dawn?

*Clare Noall  (10)*
*St Paul's CP Junior School, Penzance*




## TO A DAFFODIL

Plants bow down to the golden flower,
It stands so tall with all its power,
To a plant it's like its mother,
More beautiful than any other,
The golden flower is standing high,
As if trying to reach the sky,
The proud flower is standing strong,
But unfortunately the petals don't last long.

*Martin Nicholls  (10)*
*St Paul's CP Junior School, Penzance*

## DAFFODILS

Where the daffodils and the wind are,
I saw them dancing,
Dancing in a row,
Swaying with the wind,
The way the south wind blows,
Where the daffodils and the dew are,
In the morning light,
They are out of sight,
Spring is over.

*Jennifer Deponeo (11)*
*St Paul's CP Junior School, Penzance*


## THE WRITER OF THIS POEM

The writer of this poem,
Is as pretty as a rose,
As light as a feather,
And as soppy as a Valentine's card.

As elegant as a swan
As smooth as a piece of silk,
As funny as a tickle,
As quiet as dust settling down.

The writer of this poem,
Is so soppy,
She's probably one in a million,
That's really soppy.

*Naomi Smith (10)*
*St Teath School, Bodmin*

# THE WRITER OF THIS POEM

The writer of this poem
Is cooler than a swimming pool
As happy as the sun
As clear as a glass of water.

As fast as a racehorse
As sly as a fox
As kind as a granny
As brainy as an ant.

As gentle as a shire horse
As quick as a squirrel
As strong as a giant
As romantic as a candle.

Maybe the writer of this poem
has told one lie too many
but the writer of this poem
has told the truth now
and the writer of this poem
is worth more than all
the money in the world.

*Jenna Commins  (10)*
*St Teath School, Bodmin*

# THE WRITER OF THIS POEM

The writer of this poem
Is as strong as a rock
As small as a mouse
As skilful as a tiger.

As happy as a hyena
As clever as a brain
As crazy as a worm
As cold as an ice block.

As fast as a cheetah  ·
As fat as a pig
As chattery as a parrot
As tricky as a magician.

The writer of this poem . . .
You're as gullible as a dog
The writer of this poem
Never tells the truth.

*Lauren Sandercock  (9)*
*St Teath School, Bodmin*

# THIS IS THE EAR

This is the ear that heard a noise
that came from a cave
in the middle of the night.

This is the ear that couldn't hear
had an infection
had to have an injection.

This is the ear that went on a walk
got very cold
and started to ache.

This is the ear
that heard a noise
that had an infection
and started to ache
this is the ear that
belongs to me!

*Lucy Blewett  (10)*
*St Teath School, Bodmin*


## THE WRITER OF THIS POEM

The writer of this poem is crazy as a maniac,
as keen as a yak,
as cool as a hippy,
as mean as a nippy dog,
as brave as a mongoose,

as fast as a cheetah,
as tall as a giant,
as cool as a rabbit,
as strong as a sumo wrestler,
as flowery as a flower,

as gullible as a human,
as handsome as a meerkat,
as funny as a comedy.
The writer of this poem is me.

*Tanya Mountain  (10)*
*St Teath School, Bodmin*

## DANCING DOLPHINS

Dolphins swimming in the sea
Splashing through the waves
Dancing, jumping, leaping
and hiding by the caves.

Spraying water everywhere
Playing in the sun
Twirling, swirling, spinning
forever having fun.

Flying through the ocean
As fast as they can go
Skimming, bouncing, singing
swimming high and low.

I'd like to be a dolphin
Swimming in the sea
Splashing, squirting, twisting
always to stay free.

*Daniel Ede (10)*
*St Teath School, Bodmin*


## LIGHT AND DARK TANKA

Stars out, home at last.
Dark shadows twinkling tonight.
Inside, warm and bright.
Firelight flickering at me.
Smoke climbing up the chimney.

*Sam Langford (9)*
*Shortlanesend CP School*

## LIGHT AND DARK TANKA

The fire is calling
The flash of light leads the way
The light disappears
Then darkness comes over me
Soon be home in the warm light.

*Paul Falconbridge  (7)*
*Shortlanesend CP School*


## LIGHT AND DARK TANKA

Star star there's a star.
A very shimmery star.
Skies are very dark.
The moon is shining brightly.
The house is bright with the light.

*Fay Nicholls  (8)*
*Shortlanesend CP School*


## LIGHT AND DARK TANKA

Lonely dark night-time.
Glittering in the moonlight.
The shimmering night.
Silvery balls of bright light.
Twinkling paths of moon dust.

*Jane Grylls  (8)*
*Shortlanesend CP School*

## LIGHT AND DARK TANKA

It is dark and dim.
The dark is scary sometimes.
Light comes shining bright.
It is light, the stars shining.
The stars are shimmering still.

*Thomas Duncan  (7)*
*Shortlanesend CP School*


## LIGHT AND DARK TANKA

Light light shines brightly,
Stars twinkle in midnight sky
The sun is shining bright
Light gleaming on the sand
The sun goes the moon arrives.

*Thomas Hinkley  (7)*
*Shortlanesend CP School*


## LIGHT AND DARK TANKA

Light shines from cat's eye.
Dark shadows shine from cat's mouth.
Light shines from cat's teeth.
The cat walks into the light.
The cat sits and falls asleep.

*Richard Holroyd  (7)*
*Shortlanesend CP School*

## Light And Dark Tanka

Silver light night-time.
Glowing globe of the moonlight.
Golden waterfalls.
Golden waterfall glimmers.
Darkness conquers light today.

*Luke Hegarty  (9)*
*Shortlanesend CP School*


## A Morning In Spring

The year is at spring
The day is at morn
The blackbird at wing
As the huntsman blows his horn
The dawn is at seven
The hillside dew-pearled
It seems like heaven
Just listen to the world!

Feel that cold, damp air
That's lying everywhere
Smell that salty breeze
Listen to the birds
Nesting in the trees
As the sun rises
Silhouettes appear
Hear the song of the thrush
Spring is definitely here.

*Tim Ballingal  (10)*
*Treliske Preparatory School*

## THE DAY THE SNOW CAME

The flakes so white,
So gently they quiver,
In the night,
The animals shiver.

The morning has come,
The sky clouds clear,
Here comes the sun,
Does the blue sky appear?

The curtains depart,
Oh what delight,
Come on downstairs,
A snowball fight.

The door is flung wide,
The snow is up high,
The children in stride,
The clothes are still dry.

Such a perfect day.
The snow begins to thaw,
The day has come to an end,
The snowflakes are no more.

*Ben Ackner (10)*
*Treliske Preparatory School*

## THE PANTHER'S KILL

The panther's sleek black body
Is hiding under the bush
Waiting
Silently waiting.

A deer ran to the clearing
The panther's ears pricked up
Listening
Silently listening.

Panther saw his chance
He pounced
Hoping
Silently hoping.

The deer quick
Scaring the birds
Running
Silently running.

Out scuttled a quail
Panther cunningly jumped
Smiling
Silently smiling.

Panther silently made his kill
Pleased to have his dinner
Grinning
Silently grinning.

*Marie Powers  (10)*
*Treliske Preparatory School*

# THE MORNING SUN

A glistening sparkle peeked
from behind the clouds,
As bright as white,
As calm as still.

It rose up high,
Till light appeared,
It dazzled in the atmosphere,
As bright as white,
As calm as still.

The colours came,
To my amazement,
It was the sun,
That dazzled in the atmosphere,
As bright as white,
As calm as still.

The sun that glistened and sparkled
and peeked from behind the clouds,
As bright as white,
As calm as still,
Welcoming the morning in.

*Natalie Gadsby  (10)*
*Treliske Preparatory School*


# WHO HAD BRAVED THE STORM?

The sea was roaring,
at my feet.
The rain was pouring,
instead of heat.
The wind was howling,
in my ears.

The ships were sinking,
quick and fast.
The mothers were thinking
of their sons' past.
The fishermen who had dared,
would now be lost.

*Rebecca Wills-Devlin (10)*
*Treliske Preparatory School*


# A VISIT TO THE VET

My two cats are Siamese,
They really are quite clever.
'Let's go for a trip today,' I said.
Hoping they would agree.

'I'm not falling for that again,'
'Neither am I,' they said.
I ran to get them, sure as fate,
But the pair had started to flee.

They rushed into the aviary,
Giving the parrot a fright,
The guinea pigs jumped into the pond,
The ducks flew out for miles.

They crashed into the flowerpots,
And headed for the house,
Dad tossed them into the basket green,
Then warned the vet of our coming.

My brother surveyed the damage,
The garden was complete havoc,
Because of all their escapades,
Without them, *life would be dull!*

*Rachael O'Rourke (10)*
*Treliske Preparatory School*

## ALL ALONE ON A STORMY BEACH

Standing on a stormy shore,
The sea is pale and grey,
Today's been a real bore,
No one's come out to play.

The roar of the wind goes past my ear,
Waves seem to reach the sky,
A circus tent is on the pier,
Seagulls flying way up high.

Standing on a stormy shore,
Plainly without a care,
Standing on a stormy beach,
Just refusing any care.

The rain is pouring on my back,
The wind is whistling too,
Hail is banging on my back,
My friends need a mac too.

The wind and rain are dying down,
The ice-cream van is coming now,
Children running from the town,
The wind has gone so fast, but how?

*Thomas Kendall (10)*
*Treliske Preparatory School*

## SEASONS CHANGING

Winter's coming,
Spring is near,
Summer's leaving,
Autumn's here.

Golden leaves begin to fall
Red berries start to drop.
Then a cloak of purest white,
Brings autumn to a stop!
That was autumn!

Winter's here!
Snow's appearing,
Chilly winds begin to blow,
Frosty leaves are clearing.
That was winter!

Trees are blossoming,
Snow begins to thaw,
A tiny rabbit,
Stretches out its paw.
That was spring!

Tiny buds burst open wide,
Daffodils expand,
All the little boys and girls,
Are playing on the sand
That was summer!

*Katherine Ffrench Constant (10)*
*Treliske Preparatory School*

## PARLIAMENTARY PANDEMONIUM!

In Parliament one day,
There was a discussion in which to say
Whether to aim for world domination
Or perhaps not.

Hague and Blair didn't agree,
Hague said everyone should be free,
Blair said 'No! I'll rule them all!'
Said Hague, 'Say hello to England's downfall!'

'You're criticising my plan of plans?
*You're* not Prime Minister, baby-faced man!
So all the decisions are up to *me*,
Do you understand now? Do you see?'

Hague retorted with 'Donkey head!'
Yelled Blair, 'I'll make you regret what you said!'
And with that he picked up and hurled a grenade
At poor, defenceless William Hague.

Defenceless? Sorry, slip of the tongue!
A miniature land mine, William flung
Straight at Tony Blair.

The Speaker stood to join in the fun,
Shot half the house with her great machine gun!
One hour later, silence reigned,
It seems that only death had gained!

*Jessica Jones (11)*
*Treliske Preparatory School*

## ALL ON A WINTER DAY

I slowly awoke,
Then I got up,
I looked out of the window,
What a great sight,
Came to my eyes,
The ground was covered in snow,
I quickly got dressed,
Pulled on my boots,
Wrapped myself up,
My scarf in a loop,
Jumped out the door,
Hurdled the gate,
Ran down the lane,
Skidded to a stop,
Walked up a drive,
Knocked on a door,
And to my surprise,
A man looked out,
Better be careful because,
Grandpa's about!

*Lauren Pattison (10)*
*Treliske Preparatory School*

# WHY BOTHER WITH WAR?

Why bother with war?
People just die,
Nuclear missiles zip through the sky.

Why bother with war?
Even world domination,
Hundreds of evacuees waiting at the station.

Why bother with war?
Prisoners in pain,
Like World War Two all over again.

Why bother with war?
Bandages and First Aid,
Mortal wounds made by gun or grenade.

Why bother with war?
Broken families cried,
Praying for some loved ones that died.

Why bother with war?
Panic and terror,
It won't happen again, ever.

I bothered with war
I shot with machine gun,
I missed all the really good fun.

Don't bother with war,
Don't nearly die,
Don't fire missiles up through the sky.

*David Warman (10)*
*Treliske Preparatory School*

## THE TIGER

No one disturbs him
No one would dare.
No one would cross him
Or enter his lair.
He caught a deer
Killed it with one bite.
It died in an instant,
Petrified with fright.
He ripped up the deer
And ate it on the spot.
Then lay down to rest
Like a baby in a cot.

*Richard Vale  (10)*
*Treliske Preparatory School*


## TITANIC

Built in Belfast in 1911,
she truly was a ship from heaven.
At 11.40 on that awful night,
the thousands on board were given a fright.

People running, shouting and screaming,
the boilers and pistons and stokers were steaming.
Fifteen hundred people were killed,
and the lucky survivors were certainly chilled.

The gigantic Titanic was built to last,
and now she is gone, sunk in the past.

*John Crossley  (11)*
*Treviske CP School*

# TITANIC

Titanic was built in Belfast.
She was supposed to be built to last.
She was to sail the seven seas,
Hundreds of passengers to please.
No one was to know her fate,
Until it was far too late.

Dark, murky and cold was the night.
Titanic was a fantastic lit-up sight.
Suddenly she hit an iceberg.
A great creaking crashing sound was heard.
People, frightened, screaming and panicking found,
That Titanic was drifting down.

The passengers were jumping for life and hoping to float,
And wanting to be picked up by a boat.
Women are widows and men are dead.
Children are frightened land filled with dread
The rescuers are coming near,
To save the people and stop their fear.

*Katie Nichols (11)*
*Treviske CP School*

# THINGS I DID IN THE HOLIDAYS!

I went for a walk in the countryside,
With my step-mum at my side,
It was nice and sunny but in my
Tummy a sharp pain came,
Then we walked home and
The same thing happened again.

*Shaun Patrick Machin (10)*
*Treviske CP School*

# THE LOSS OF THE HUMAN RACE

On the cold dreadful night
when the biggest dream sank,
the death toll was enormous,
and so was she.

The Titanic the unsinkable ship
so they thought.
The stairs, the chandeliers
are all now filled with
small sea life.

The bow of the ship
now rusted away,
in the freezing cold waters
of the North Atlantic.

Their friends, their families
some still alive
and some at rest,
on this bed of
the merciful depths.

The treasures which it held
within its gigantic hull,
the majority of those
people of that decade
now live on the seabed.

*Jeremy Anderson  (10)*
*Treviske CP School*

## A POEM ABOUT POETRY

I love poetry -
Don't you?
I like the rhyming.
I like the timing.
Don't you?

You can express
Your feelings,
Or you can protect
Your feelings,
Don't you think
That's pretty great?

You can write about water,
You can write about your
Mum's other daughter.
Or you can write about
Something great -
Something small -
Just about anything at all!

*Abigail Stevens  (10)*
*Treviske CP School*


## THE LOSS OF LIFE

I remember the loss of life
People shouting with fear,
the stars in the sky shining brightly
the sinking was near.

People rushing around,
falling into the murky sea,
the iceberg still
and as cold as could be.

Lifeboats splashing down
people trying to keep calm,
the Titanic is going,
going, going, gone.

*Hannah Simpson (11)*
*Treviske CP School*


## TITANIC DISASTER

Water came pouring in my mind
Then I turned around to find
It wasn't just my mind at all
It was the ship sinking at nightfall.

'Oh, help, help, I'm drowning here!
Don't any of you have ears?'
I finally clung onto a seat
And climbed back onto my own two feet.

Water was sliding across the floor
And was making its way to the door
I was trapped on the back of the ship
Hearing a snap, I accidentally tripped.

The door burst open, with a cry
I got up and then I dived
My father swept me up in his arms
And all I can remember was the water on my palms.

I woke up looking at something quite bright
Then I realised it wasn't that light
The thing was sinking down, down
And I am glad I didn't drown!

*Carly Prescott (11)*
*Treviske CP School*

# TITANIC

A floating dream that turned into a sinking
nightmare.
A day when a roller-coaster ride seemed like a joke.
Children who had no chance to live.
The orchestra who stayed there until the end.
The iceberg that stood in the wrong place,
and the captain, the strongest of them all.

The survivors who were strong,
the people that froze, froze, froze to death.
People that didn't even know the ship was sinking.
Survivors who had to live with their treasures
under the water.
But Titanic is alive, oh yes very alive.
Until the clock stops, stops, stops.

*Rebecca Skinner (10)*
*Treviske CP School*


# MY DIARY

When I was on the Titanic
I began to panic.
When the sand washed around the boat
my body became afloat.
When the birds began to fly
my heart began to cry.
That captain must be insane
to cause so much pain.
When I fell
I felt as though I was going to hell.

*Philip Hicks (10)*
*Treviske CP School*

# TITANIC

Deep under the sea the Titanic lies
Lost in a world of its own.
The shots rang out, the widows cried,
For the men left to die alone.

But Titanic is alive, very much alive,
And will be until the end of time,
Until the day the clock thirteen does chime,
The Titanic will rise again, again.

And sail with the band and Captain Smith
Who owns again the humbling myth
Whose fate was sealed,
And rolled and reeled,
And took a final plunge to the deep.

Now Titanic is queen of the deep Atlantic
And we all remember the feeling of panic
Locked inside the ship as we found
With her we were going down, down.

Down here we are now, all that's left is our shoes
We wander and roam the sea as we choose
And we all remember that fateful day
When so many people drifted away.

*Kate Neale (11)*
*Treviske CP School*

# DEATH AT DAWN

The giant ship of dreams one day,
sailed oh so far away,
not to know its death ahead,
people waking from their bed.

It sailed through the deep Atlantic,
no one knows the great sense of panic,
except for people who were there, like me,
they were the only ones to see, the great Titanic sink.

'Woman and children first' they called,
no men though, none at all,
wives crying, people dying,
children screaming, people still sleeping, dreaming.

The stern went up, the bow went down,
people's faces turned to frowns,
this screaming terrible night I hope,
will never ever happen again.

*Kelly Young  (11)*
*Treviske CP School*


## PLUTO

Pluto is grey,
The furthest away,
Away from the sun,
Leaving no trace just circling space.

Its moon sometimes comes,
Between it and the sun,
Yet it does not know,
That its name is Pluto.

*Natalie Callow  (10)*
*Treviske CP School*

# A WASTE OF LIVES

Alexander Carlie designed her to last
But the captain was going too fast,
2,300 people were screaming
As water was coming from the ceiling.

People were rushing for a boat
Or throwing things in the water hoping to float
Many people knew they would die
People on lifeboats waving goodbye.

Everyone lost someone that night,
People that lived, remembered that horrid sight,
On the bottom of the ocean the Titanic will stay
With the silent screaming passengers where they lay.

*Sarah Connolly (11)*
*Treviske CP School*


# DOWN AND OUT

Titanic, tilting vertically,
People slipping and sliding,
Falling over the edge, drowning,
Dying, hold in your fear.
The unsinkable is sinking
Gulping down
All the children have to be found
Screaming, shouting fills the air.
'Oh no! We're in the iceberg field.'
Smack, bang, crack.
Now the ship is in two
The funnels disappearing into the deep blue
Rowing to get away
From the suction zone.

*Aaron Hawken (10)*
*Treviske CP School*

## ICY GRAVEYARD

'Man overboard!' I heard someone cry,
not knowing whether she was going to die.
People running from their berths below,
to lifeboats that overflow.

'Over here, this one is free!'
I heard someone call to me.
I ran over determined to fight,
the other people in the lifeboat's sight.

I sailed away,
leaving my father to stay.
Leaving the life of mankind behind,
with the ruins of the Titanic people might find.

The Christmas card background,
*Unsinkable Titanic* vanishes without a sound.
Suddenly everything went silent,
the Titanic went down with violence.

*Claire Strafford (11)*
*Treviske CP School*

## DREAMING!

As I lay down on the soft mattress,
I drift away into a dream,
Dreaming about imaginary places and imaginary things,
As the dream drifts away I toss and turn,
As a nightmare comes I breathe heavily in and out,
Now I'm awake and the nightmare has gone!

*Carly Edwards (10)*
*Treviske CP School*

## BEING ON TITANIC

Rocking gently on the sea
Titanic is the place for me
The great big lovely sights
Shining in the starry night.

Suddenly, there was a crash
Cling, clang, crash, bash!
Icebergs were on the deck
Some were up to people's necks.

Officers were putting the lifeboats down
I started to panic I thought I would drown
Titanic was starting to sink
It was going down in every blink.

I was in a lifeboat I was okay
On that horrible, horrible, horrible day
The Carpathia came and picked us up
I jumped for joy up and up.

*Alex Fairhurst (10)*
*Treviske CP School*


## DRAGON POEM

Fiery
Wings of destruction,
Magnificent sights in the pitch-black nights,
Deep red eyes like pools of blood,
Talons of death come down from the heavens.

A path of destruction is led through the land,
As the great and almighty soar high and grand.

*Darryl Smale (11)*
*Treviske CP School*

## THE WIND ON THE HEATHER

The wind on the heather is wild and free,
Those miserable Romans won't beat me,
I'll thrash them and kill them 'til they're no more,
Death will fall upon them.

With my sword by my side,
And my bare arms cold,
I go out to battle,
I hope I'm bold!

The death-threatening wind,
The old grey stone,
Hadrian's wall,
Stands alone.

I spy a young wall-soldier,
Looking glum,
Why am I doing this,
Is it for fun?

He doesn't like war,
And neither do I,
A point of doing this,
'No.' I sigh.

War is such a horrid thing,
I look at the sky in shame,
War is such a horrid thing,
Do we have to do it again?

*Alexander Beadel (10)*
*Treviske CP School*